I0486518

Common Sense Investing

by
Lyle Allen

Bloomington, IN  Milton Keynes, UK

AuthorHouse™
1663 Liberty Drive, Suite 200
Bloomington, IN 47403
www.authorhouse.com
Phone: 1-800-839-8640

AuthorHouse™ UK Ltd.
500 Avebury Boulevard
Central Milton Keynes, MK9 2BE
www.authorhouse.co.uk
Phone: 08001974150

© 2006 Lyle Allen. All rights reserved.

No part of this book may be reproduced, stored in a retrieval system, or
transmitted by any means without the written permission of the author.

First published by AuthorHouse 7/25/2006

ISBN: 1-4259-4187-7 (sc)

Printed in the United States of America
Bloomington, Indiana

This book is printed on acid-free paper.

DISCLAIMER

This self-help product is intended to be used by the consumer for his or her own benefit. It may not be reproduced in whole or in part, resold or used for commercial purposes without the written consent of the publisher.

This product is designed to provide accurate information in regard to the subject matter covered. However, the accuracy of the information is not guaranteed, as laws and regulations may change or be subject to different interpretations. Consequently, you may be responsible for following alternative procedures, or using material different from that offered with this product.

Neither the author, publisher, distributor nor retailer are engaged in rendering legal, investment or other professional advice. Accordingly, the publisher, author, distributor and retailer shall have neither liability nor responsibility to any party for any loss or damage caused or alleged to be caused by the use of this product.

COPYRIGHT NOTICE

The purchaser of this product is hereby authorized to reproduce in any form or by any means, all forms and documents contained in this product, provided it is for non-profit, educational or private use. The reproduction of any form or document contained in this product intended for sale is prohibited without the written permission of the publisher.

TABLE OF CONTENTS

INTRODUCTION

Making money when you invest does not involve calling your broker everyday, trading actively, or switching frequently among investments. The smart investor is the one who makes a plan, selects the right investments to implement the plan and gives it time to work. Whether you are a beginner or experienced investor, this book can help you profit in the financial markets and reach your goals, whatever they are. If you want to save for the down payment on a house, provide for your children's college, supplement your retirement income, or put aside money for something else, this book can help you.

The best way to get a head start on your goals is to have an investment plan. This book shows you how to evaluate your current financial situation and develop an investment plan. If you already have a plan, this book will help you determine whether it is adequate to reach your goals.

The theme of this book is that mutual funds should be included in most investment plans. Mutual funds are a convenient way to invest in stocks, bonds, or the money market without doing too much work. Although several types of mutual funds are available, open-end, no-load funds are specially emphasized. These funds offer a convenient way to invest, and many provide a good return on investors' money.

The mutual fund industry has grown through the years into a nearly $7 trillion business with over seven thousand funds. They employ professional managers, require a relatively small amount to open an account, and provide an array of shareholder services. An attractive feature of mutual funds is that federal and state laws regulate what they can and cannot do with investors' money. Funds must make a thorough disclosure of their operations to the Securities and Exchange Commission, state regulators, and their shareholders.

This book points out the advantages and disadvantages of investing in mutual funds, where to get information on funds, and how to choose a fund. Best of all, this book shows you how to invest in mutual funds using the Dollar-Cost Averaging Plus (DCAP) formula. It requires that you invest monthly and that you vary the amount of your investment in relation to a target price. The formula can greatly increase the return on your investments in a fund.

You will learn about the advantages and disadvantages of investing in stocks as well as funds; how to assess annuities, real estate, unit trusts, limited partnerships, bonds, and other investments; and how to build an investment portfolio that's right for you.

The key to investment success is to have a sound financial plan. So this book will show you how to identify basic family needs that should be met before you start to invest, how to take a financial inventory, reduce your living expenses, and find ways to save and invest regularly.

You will be shown how to tie everything together in a financial plan that has direction, priorities, and the potential to produce a sizeable nest egg for your special goals.

This book is primarily for the person who wants to manage his or her own investments without the aid of full-service stockbrokers, insurance agents, or financial planners. Managing your own investments isn't easy, but it can be very rewarding. It requires time, patience, and, most of all a desire to succeed.

CHAPTER 1
BEFORE YOU INVEST

Few people would drive to New York without first looking at a road map to determine the best way to get there. You should apply the same principle before you invest. It's to your advantage to identify your goals and develop a road map or plan before you make any investment decisions.

You can set goals, develop a plan, and reach investment decisions yourself, without the use of a full-service broker, insurance agent, or financial planner. Keep in mind that anyone who provides help on your finances will charge for the service, usually a very steep charge.

SETTING GOALS

The most successful investment plans are those with a sense of purpose—a goal. Unless you have worthy goals to achieve, your plan lacks direction. You probably can't afford all your goals at once, so decide which are most important and work to achieve those first.

What is a worthy goal? It involves saving for a future event that has a realistic objective and a dollar amount. Some of the more popular goals are:

* Save for a major purchase.
* Save for a vacation.

1

* Provide for your children's education.

* Save for the down payment on a house.

* Start your own business.

* Supplement your retirement income.

List Your Goals

Make a list of your goals. Decide the date you expect to achieve them and how much they are going to cost. The cost of some goals may be difficult to assess, because taxes, inflation, and unexpected emergencies will affect your financial situation over the years.

If your goal is to invest to pay for college expenses, for example, estimate the total amount you will need. To arrive at that estimate, you will have to make assumptions such as the increase in tuition costs, books, housing, recreation, and increases (or decreases) in your family's income. You must also decide on the investment risk you feel comfortable with, and calculate the amount you need to save monthly to reach your goal.

After you list your goals, classify them as either short-, medium-, or long-term. This distinction is important because it determines which securities to include in your investment plan.

Short-Term Goals

Short-term goals are the ones you want to attain rapidly—in less than five years. They could include the down payment on a house, a vacation, or a major purchase.

If you have some of the money you need for your short-term goals, consider securities that are not highly speculative. There is no reason to jeopardize the money you already have by making risky investments. Safe investments such as government securities, high-quality bond funds, and money market mutual funds are ideal for short-term goals. With all short-term investments, make certain their maturity date coincides with the date of your goal.

If you have no money set aside for your short-term goals, consider securities that are more speculative. These include common stocks and mutual funds.

Medium-Term Goals

With medium-term goals, you have more time and more investment choices. Maybe you would like to buy a larger house or a new car in about five or six years. Since these goals are a few years away, you could hold conservative as well as speculative investments. Investments suitable for medium-term goals are growth mutual funds, bond funds, and common stocks. As the date approaches when you'll need your money, sell your stocks and growth mutual funds and put the proceeds in a money market mutual fund. There is no need to continue with more speculative investments as your goal draws near.

Long-Term Goals

Long-term goals usually cost the most and take several years to attain. They could include funds for your children's college, money for a second home, and money to supplement your retirement. Since these goals are years away, you can be more speculative with your investments. Growth funds, common stocks, and zero-coupon bonds are good investments for long-term goals.

MONTHLY INCOME AND EXPENSES

Once you decide your goals and the time to reach them, review your current financial situation. To do that, complete the monthly income and expense worksheet below. The worksheet contains two parts. The first part is for listing basic living expenses—those that are essential and necessary. The second is for listing discretionary items—those that are nonessential and can be reduced or discontinued. The worksheet doesn't have to include exact figures. Rather, it should be a general accounting of your monthly income and expenses. After you complete the worksheet, you will be able to:

* Determine your monthly living expenses.

* Decide which discretionary items you can cut back on or drop.

3

*   Determine how much money is available for investments after you pay your bills.

MONTHLY INCOME AND EXPENSE WORKSHEET

(A) Living Expenses		(B) Discretionary Cost Items	
Housing (mortgage, rent)	------------	Credit Cards	------------
Utilities (electric, gas, water, phone)	------------	Clothing	------------
Food	------------	Personal care (barber, beauty parlor, cosmetics, cleaners)	------------
Medical expenses	------------	Books, newspapers, magazines	
		Transportation	------------
Insurance (life, health, auto, house, rental)	------------	Travel	------------
Other	------------	Education	------------
		Entertainment	------------
		Gifts	------------
		Other	------------

Totals: (A) ------------   (B) -------------

Monthly net income   ------------

Less total of columns A and B   ------------

Money available for investing   ------------

REDUCING LIVING EXPENSES

The most obvious benefit of the monthly income and expense worksheet is that it shows you where your money is being spent. In addition, it can help you reduce your monthly expenses and locate money for investments. You may be surprised at how much your expenses can be cut if you really try.

Look at your living expenses in column A on the worksheet. Go over the items to see if you can reduce them. Here are some ideas on how you can make reductions.

Housing

* If you have a house mortgage, see whether you can extend the payment period. For example, extend a twenty-five-year mortgage to thirty years to reduce payments.

* If your mortgage is higher than prevailing rates, refinance at a lower rate.

* Check with whoever holds your mortgage to see if your escrow account has excess money that you could withdraw.

* If you are a renter, consider moving to a unit that has lower rent than what you now pay.

Utilities

* Calk and weatherstrip the doors and windows on your house or apartment. Make sure your attic insulation meets your state's code.

* Install an insulation blanket on your water heater. Adjust the thermostat on your water heater for the season—lower in the summer, higher in the winter.

* Use ceiling fans to circulate the air in your house or apartment.

* Install shades and drapes in your house or apartment to keep cold air outside and warm air inside. .On your refrigerator, clean the coils, make certain the doors close tightly, and adjust the temperature for the season.

* Use a clothesline to dry clothes rather than an electric dryer.

* Replace 100-watt light bulbs with 60-watt bulbs. When you leave a room in your house or apartment, turn off the lights.

* Make fewer long-distance telephone calls. Sign up for a special

rate reduction plan sponsored by most long-distance carriers.

* Water your lawn and flowers in the evening. During the daytime hours, much of the water evaporates.

Food

* At the supermarket, buy store-brand foods that cost less.

* Buy your groceries at discount food warehouses where prices are usually lower than at supermarkets.

* Shop for groceries less often to avoid impulse buying.

* Buy staple groceries in bulk and store them to avoid inflationary pricing.

* Save and use food discount coupons.

Medical

* Since brand name drugs are usually more expensive than their generic equivalents, ask your physician or pharmacist for generic drugs whenever appropriate.

* Pharmacies may charge widely different prices for the same medicine, so contact several to compare prices.

* Consider a mail order pharmacy which may charge lower prices than your local pharmacy.

Insurance

* If you have to pay part or all of your health and accident insurance, shop for a plan that has the same benefits at less cost.

* Health and accident insurance usually costs less when purchased under a group policy rather than individually, so consider buying health and accident insurance where you work.

* If you are like many people, you could have too much life insurance. For most young families, term insurance that is less costly than permanent insurance, may be adequate.

* If you purchase a permanent insurance policy, plan to hold it for several years. Canceling these policies after only a few years

can more than double your life insurance costs.

REDUCING DISCRETIONARY COST ITEMS

Now look at your discretionary items in column B of the worksheet. This is where you can reduce many costs. Some things to consider are these.

Clothing

* Avoid buying clothes on impulse. Use a buying list when you shop for clothes and stick to it.

* Shop for clothes at designer outlets, off-price stores, and factory outlets where apparel usually costs less than at department stores.

* Before you pay a high price for a tuxedo or formal dress that you may seldom wear, check the cost to rent one.

* Plan and coordinate your wardrobe. For example, men can purchase a sports coat that goes with more than one pair of slacks, and women can buy shoes that go with more than one dress.

Personal care

* Make fewer trips to the beauty salon or barber shop to cut expenses.

* With today's new fabrics and spot removers, you can reduce dry cleaning costs.

* Buy wash and wear clothes to save on dry cleaning costs.

Books, newspapers, and magazines

* Ask yourself, is all the reading material I buy necessary? Do I read all the publications to which I subscribe?

* Use the library more often. A good library carries most of the better publications.

Transportation

* If you borrow money to buy an auto, check with more than one

finance source to get the lowest possible rate on your loan.

* Since you cannot deduct interest on an auto loan from your taxes, it's better to pay cash when you buy an auto. If that isn't possible, instead of buying a new auto, you can buy a nearly new one. There are many, one to two-year-old autos that have low mileage and are still under warranty.

* You can save hundreds of dollars over the lifetime of an auto by selecting one that combines a low purchase price with low financing, insurance, and repair costs.

Travel

* Rather than driving your auto to and from work, you can save money by taking the subway, van pooling, or riding the bus. Public transportation is usually less expensive than driving your auto.

* When you travel out of town, use no-fee travel checks, budget motels, airline discount fares, frequent flyer miles, and compare prices.

* Long vacation trips away from home can be costly. Instead of a two-week trip, limit your time to one week. Spend the second week in short, less costly trips close to home.

Education

* You can realize substantial savings by choosing a public over a private school for your children's education.

* Buy school supplies when they are off-season, at discount stores, and when they are on sale.

* If eligible, your children can apply for college grants, scholarships, and work-study programs to reduce education costs.

* Open a 529 Plan which allows you to either prepay tuition for qualified colleges or save money in a tax-free account for college costs.

Entertainment

* Host fewer parties during the year.

* Occasionally serve wine at parties instead of more expensive liquor.

* Go less frequently to plays, movies, costly restaurants, and social affairs.

Gifts

* In January, make a list of the people you expect to give gifts to during the year. Then buy the gifts when they are on sale.

* Avoid buying gifts a few days before Christmas when prices are usually higher.

* Wait until after the holidays to buy next year's Christmas gifts when the cost of many items is less.

Other ways to cut expenses

Compare products and prices at several stores before you buy to get the best product at the lowest price. Cancel your high cost health club membership and exercise at home or in the park. Consider carefully all of your cash contributions to charities, especially if you cannot deduct them from your taxes.

These are some of the ways to reduce living and discretionary cost items. Your aim should be to search for ways to cut your expenses, to free more money for investing.

One way to use the monthly income and expense worksheet is to set aside a specific amount each month for investing after living expenses are paid. Then apportion the remainder of your monthly income among your discretionary items. This is called paying yourself first—before you spend money for nonessential items.

CREDIT CARD REVIEW

As many people know, there are several ways to get into debt. Most people use mortgage debt when they buy a house, and borrow to finance the purchase of an automobile. These are useful ways to purchase essential living needs.

The trouble with debt is that it can get out of control and become a problem before many borrowers even realize it. Probably the easiest way for debt to become a problem is with the excess use of credit cards. Credit card interest rates generally range from an annual percentage rate (APR) of 12 percent to 21 percent. If you must borrow money on a credit card, get one that charges a low interest rate. What's more, if your credit card charges a high annual fee, switch to one with a low fee. Consider any amount over $25 a year as high.

It shouldn't be difficult to see how credit card debt could place a burden on your finances. The burden results from the large amount of money you can borrow and the high interest charged by the lender. If you want to avoid financial trouble, then control the use of your credit cards.

You can decide if your credit card debt is getting out of control by completing the credit card worksheet below. It will only take a few minutes, and it could be well worth the time spent. For simplicity, you should combine your credit debt on the worksheet.

CREDIT CARD WORKSHEET

Type of Card	Total Amount Borrowed	Interest Rate	Outstanding Balance	Monthly Payments
_____	_____	_____	_____	_____
1. _____	_____	_____	_____	_____
2. _____	_____	_____	_____	_____
3. _____	_____	_____	_____	_____
4. _____	_____	_____	_____	_____
5. _____	_____	_____	_____	_____
Totals	_____	_____	_____	_____

Appraisal:

(A) Monthly net income $ ------------

(B) Total monthly credit card payments $ ------------

(C) B divided by A = ----------- percent of net income used to pay credit card debt

If C is greater than 20 percent, credit card debt may be out of control.

Reviewing the Credit Card Worksheet

Let's look at the credit card worksheet. Compare your total credit card payments on the worksheet and on the monthly income and expense worksheet. The amounts should be the same. Credit debt is on the credit card worksheet so that you know what percent of your monthly income goes for credit and on the income and expense worksheet as a discretionary item, which means you can do something to reduce your debt.

On the credit card worksheet, look at the interest rates you pay lenders for borrowing money. Are there any under 15 percent APR? Compare the lender's rates with interest earned on a one-year certificate of deposit (CD) at a local bank. The difference between the two rates is probably 10 percent to 12 percent for the lender. It's no secret that the credit business is very profitable for the lender and a burden for the borrower.

Now total your outstanding card debt and divide it by the total of all your monthly credit card payments. The result is the number of months it will take to pay your outstanding debt, assuming there are no more charges.

If you use over 20 percent of your net income to pay for credit card debt, you could be headed for financial trouble. The 20 percent figure, of course, is only a guideline.

There is no doubt that credit card debt is a financial burden, unless the balance is paid within the card issuer's grace period. The uncontrolled use of these cards can push you deep into debt. Fortunately, you can do something to eliminate credit card debt.

Eliminating Credit Card Debt

The first action you can take to eliminate credit card debt is to limit the number of cards you own. Most people do not need to have more than three to four cards. One or two cards for business and travel expenses and one or two retail cards should be enough.

Second, if your outstanding card debt is at a high interest rate, try to pay it off with a bank or credit union loan at a lower rate. Thus, combine all your debt into a new loan at a lower interest rate. Switching from an 18 percent interest rate to a rate of 12 percent will save you about $34 for each $1,000 of balance you carry, if you pay it off in a year.

Third, avoid applying for department store credit cards, since they often have higher interest rates than standard credit cards.

Finally, assume no new credit card debt. When your current debt is paid off, pay any new bills within thirty days so no finance charges will accrue.

It's always possible that an illness or the loss of your job may prevent you from paying your credit card debt on time. Should you have a problem with your debt, try to work out a modified payment plan with your credit card company. Although it's probably better to modify (or rebuild) your credit with the help of a financial consulting firm, bank, credit union, or another responsible party. This is viewed by the credit card company as the first sign of your willingness to repay your debt.

If you have credit card problems, the Consumer Credit Counseling Service (CCCS) may be able to help you. This non-profit organization with more than700 offices in the United States will try to arrange a debt payment plan that is acceptable to you and the credit card company. You can obtain the address of the CCCS office nearest to you by contacting:

National Foundation for Credit Counseling

801 Roeder Road

Silver Spring, MD 20910

Telephone: 1-800-388-2227

www.nfcc.org

If you are going to build a good financial plan, one that will help you save a meaningful amount each month, you must exercise control over the use of your credit cards. Remember, it's difficult to save objectively when you worry about debt.

FAMILY EXPENSE RECORD

One way to manage your money is to keep a family expense record. An expense record is a guide to spending that will enable you to take control of your finances, live within your income, and set aside some savings.

An expense record can be stimulating, challenging, and prove very profitable. All that's needed is to: first, account for what percent of your income goes for each expense item; and second, project what percent each expense item will be reduced. Once you become accustomed to an expense record, you'll probably find that it's not only easy to maintain but you can better manage your finances.

If you start an expense record, it is a good idea to involve all family members. Only when all members participate, can you get good results. An expense record is useless if one family member follows the record and another goes on a spending spree. Before you start an expense record, here is a short quiz to see if you really need one.

* Do you have trouble paying your bills on time?
* If you have credit debt, is the balance increasing or decreasing?
* Are you using cash advances on your credit cards for living expenses or to pay bills?
* Do you borrow money from friends or relatives to pay bills?

* Do you draw money from savings for daily expenses?

* Have you recently been denied credit?

If you answered yes to any of the above questions, it may be time to begin an expense record. An expense record is sometimes difficult to stick to and does require some work, but it can provide some good results.

UNDERSTANDING RISK

All investments carry a degree of risk—the chance that all or part of your money could be lost. Risk pertains not only to preserving the money that you invest but also to the return on your investments. This means that you can have relatively safe investments and still be susceptible to risk with respect to what your investments earn through interest, dividends, and capital gains.

When you invest, what are the risks? The major one is the risk that the after-tax return on your investments will not keep pace with the rate of inflation. For example, let's assume that you have a one-year CD that pays interest at 4 percent. If the rate of inflation is 4 percent, and you are in the 28 percent tax bracket, the actual return on your CD is around minus 1 percent. Thus, a CD for $1,000 would be worth only $988 at the end of the year—certainly it is not a risk-free investment, since inflation consumes 4 percent and taxes 28 percent of your money. When you invest, inflation is the biggest and most certain risk you will face.

Another kind of risk is the possibility that your investments will drop below the price you paid for them. This is called market risk, and applies equally as well to gold, art, collectibles, and real estate as it does to stocks, bonds, and mutual funds.

You can largely offset market risk if you invest for the long term in good stocks and top-rated mutual funds. How is this possible? Historically, when the stock market has dropped, it eventually has risen above its earlier level, and the price of good stocks and the better mutual funds have gone up with the market.

Since you cannot avoid risk when you invest, you need to find a way to manage risk. Before you make any investment decisions, determine the amount of risk you can accept. To help you determine this, the table below lists various investments by their level of risk and potential return. Review the investments and decide which ones you feel most comfortable with.

RELATIVE RISK AND RETURN RANKINGS

Type of Investment	Risk level	Potential Return
Government securities	Low	Medium
Municipal bonds	Low	Medium
Bank instruments	Medium	Low
Annuities	Medium	Low
Money market mutual funds	Medium	Medium
Corporate bonds	Medium	Medium
Bond mutual funds	Medium	Medium
Growth mutual funds	Medium	High
Quality growth stocks	Medium/High	High
Zero-coupon bonds	Medium/High	High
Rental real estate	High	Medium
Oil and gas limited partnerships	High	Medium
Numismatic coins	High	Medium
Commodity contracts	High	High
Futures contracts	High	High

The risk and potential return levels assigned to the investments in the table may vary according to who does the ranking, but there is a general consensus on the investments that rank at the top and bottom of the table.

The amount of risk you can handle may depend on you income and family circumstances. For example, someone with high income and no dependents usually can handle more risk than someone with relatively low income and several dependents.

Don't let risk be the only factor when you make investment decisions. Weigh the risk of an investment against its return and then consider only investments that are within your comfort level.

EMERGENCY FUND

Before you invest, set up a fund for small and unexpected emergencies. It seems that the car always needs some repairs or the house requires a few improvements when you least expect it. The most obvious reason for an emergency fund is to pay for those small and unexpected expenses. Another reason is to have money available so you won't have to sell your investments for small emergencies.

How much should you set aside in an emergency fund? The answer varies from family to family, but about three months of your net pay is the minimum amount. Today, with severance pay, unemployment insurance, company health benefits, and a growing job market, a three-month fund should be enough to cover any small emergency.

In case of a major emergency, such as the loss of a job, disabling illness, or the death of a spouse, a three-month fund probably wouldn't cover all your expenses. It's the little crises, not the big ones, that an emergency fund is useful. If a major emergency occurs, the last resource to consider is your emergency fund. Better sources to pay for a major emergency are any cash value you have accumulated in life insurance policies, borrowing against your company retirement plan, and a home equity loan.

One way to save money for an emergency is to make regular payments in a money market mutual fund (MMMF). In many ways MMMFs are like checking accounts but better, since they usually pay a higher interest rate. Most MMMFs provide free checks for use against your deposits, but the minimum amount you can write is usually $500.

A high minimum on checks is good since it could stop you from writing them for small, nonessential items.

Another way to save for an emergency is to have your bank take a deduction from your paycheck and deposit it in a savings account. Today, most savings accounts pay anywhere from 2 percent to 3 percent.

One problem with an emergency fund is that it provides you with an opportunity to call any setback an emergency and spend the money. Therefore, you'll have to distinguish between a real emergency and what is merely a cost of living expense. Setting aside money for an emergency and using it only for a bona fide emergency is an essential part of any investment plan. Remember, an emergency fund could be the difference between a good plan and one that is only ordinary.

COMPUTER-AIDED PLANNING

If you have a personal computer, it can help with your financial planning. All you need is the appropriate software package that will run on your computer.

Software packages vary by product, but many will balance checkbooks, create budgets, plan for taxes, track investments, and list expenses. Many packages have expense groupings for mortgage payments, groceries, insurance, utilities, and entertainment.

If you buy computer software to track your budget, be sure that the package provides names for different expense groupings such as housing, food, utilities, and medical. And, that you can transfer information from one month to the next in case you want to revise your financial plan. If you have outstanding loans to track, make certain you select software that adjusts your loan balance after a payment, computes interest paid, and adjusts the principal.

It should be easy to find an acceptable software package. Two packages to consider are MasterPlan and Quicken.

CHAPTER 2
INVESTMENT CHOICES

Let's imagine that you inherit $50,000 and decide to invest the whole amount. Before you rush out to invest your $50,000, match the amount of risk you can accept with the investments that are available.

Investing in gold bullion or numismatic coins, for example, is very risky. Besides, these investments do not pay interest or dividends. Also, the true value of fixed income investments such as CDs and bonds are eroded by inflation. So what should you do with your money?

Here's a list of several investments. Their advantages and disadvantages are pointed out so you can decide which are the right ones for you.

GOVERNMENT SECURITIES

The federal government offers a variety of debt securities. Many are exempt from state and local taxes, but subject to federal taxes. They are probably the safest investments available and provide an array of yields and maturity dates. Here are some government securities to consider for your investment plan.

Treasury Bills, Notes, and Bonds

Treasury bills are auctioned each week and sell at a discount to their par value, which is $10,000. If you don't have $10,000, less the discount, forget about treasury bills. They are short-term investments that mature in thirteen or twenty-six weeks.

Treasury notes sell in denominations as low as $1,000 for those that mature in two to ten years. Some other notes require a minimum of $5,000. The yield on treasury notes is comparable to the yield on treasury bills.

Treasury bonds are longer-term investments that sell in denominations of $1,000 to $5,000. Treasury bonds usually mature in excess of ten years, and some can be called in (redeemed) before their maturity date. Interest is paid semiannually and varies with each issue.

Federal Agency Securities

Federal agency securities are offered in units of $1,000 to $25,000 by government agencies such as the Federal National Mortgage Association, Government National Mortgage Association, Federal Home Loan Mortgage Corporation, and other federal agencies. They have a maturity range of from one to 40 years, and provide a greater yield to maturity than treasury securities, often a percentage point or so more. Since federal agency securities, unlike treasury securities, have no government guarantee for the payment of interest and return of principal, they carry more risk. In addition, the price of agency securities fluctuates in relation to interest rates in general so their value goes down if new issues pay more than existing ones.

If you are not comfortable investing in individual government securities, you can buy shares in a U. S. government income fund. These funds hold treasury bonds, mortgage-backed securities, and other government notes.

Series EE Bonds

Series EE bonds are sold by the U.S. Treasury in denominations of $50 to a maximum of $10,000. EE bonds earn the interest rate in effect at the time of the purchase for as long as you own the bonds. The interest is exempt from all state and local income taxes, and you can defer federal tax until the bonds mature or you redeem them. At maturity, you can exchange your Series EE bonds for Series HH bonds.

Doing this, you won't be taxed on the interest your EE bonds earned until the HH bonds reach maturity. Since Series EE bonds are backed by the U. S. government and provide an attractive yield, they might fit your investment plan.

Series I Bonds

Series I bonds are sold at face value in denominations of $50 to $30,000. I bonds are inflation indexed, which means they are designed to offer a rate of return above inflation. Interest paid on the bonds consists of two parts. One is the fixed rate, which stays the same throughout the 30-year life of the bond. The other is the inflation rate, adjusted every six months. Interest which is compounded semiannually is exempt from state and local taxes, but not federal taxes. However, federal income tax on I Bonds can be deferred until the bonds are cashed or they stop earning interest. I Bonds may be purchased from most banks or credit unions or from the Treasury at www.publicdebt.gov.

Government securities do have some good investment features. They are exempt from state and local taxes; you can replace them if they are lost; and, except for agency securities, they are backed by the federal government.

The disadvantages of investing in government securities are that, except for Series I bonds, they have a fixed rate of return; their interest is usually lower than other types of investments; there is a maturity date that makes them somewhat illiquid; they are sold in denominations that might not fit everyone's budget; and their interest is not (except for Series EE and I bonds) reinvested or compounded.

BANK INSTRUMENTS

Bank instruments include investments such as CDs, passbook savings accounts, money market deposit accounts, and interest-paying checking accounts.

Bank instruments offer certain advantages, and the first is safety. Your deposits are fully insured by the Federal Deposit Insurance Corporation up to $100,000, if the bank is covered by the organization.

Second, bank accounts are easy to open and close and there are no sales commissions for deposits or withdrawals.

The disadvantages to bank instruments include penalties for early withdrawals on time deposits; being locked into a low-paying CD when interest rates rise; the requirement of a minimum balance to receive interest on checking; and a low rate of return compared to some other investments. If you want a higher return on your money with slightly more risk, there are better investments available than what banks have to offer.

ANNUITIES

Annuities are sold primarily by life insurance companies and include two general types: single premium, which requires a large, one time sum of money, and deferred, which requires monthly, quarterly, or yearly payments. Annuities are designed to supplement your long-term savings and come in two types: fixed and variable.

Fixed Annuities

With a fixed annuity, you give your money to an insurance company which invests it for you and pays you a fixed rate of return, usually for a set period. When the period ends, the insurance company determines a new interest rate for the next period. A fixed annuity allows your money to grow at a competitive and tax-deferred rate. However, unlike variable annuities, the assets of fixed annuities are invested in the insurance company's general account and are subject to creditor's claims.

Variable Annuities

Variable annuities allow you a choice of investments, usually you have the option to invest in stock, bond, and money market mutual funds. In addition, a variable annuity will allow you to switch among investment choices tax free. However, the value of a variable annuity invested in a mutual fund will increase or decrease as the fund changes in price. You can buy variable annuities from insurance agents, financial planners, stockbrokers, and from mutual funds companies that have paired with insurers to market annuities.

The main advantage to annuities is that any interest, dividends, and capital gains paid to your account are tax-deferred. Another is that an annuity is issued by an insurance company, so your assets are passed to your estate or beneficiary as if they were insurance. Their disadvantages include high sales commissions, early withdrawal penalties, low rates of return, and, in some cases, poor management. Because annuities generally have built-in commissions and fees, before you invest in them take advantage of less expensive savings options such as an individual retirement account (IRA).

GOLD AND SILVER INVESTMENTS

Investing in gold and silver bullion or coins is very risky. At times, these investments can be a hedge against inflation, but other investments also do that.

Gold and silver bullion is bought and sold in relation to the price of the metals in the world market. These prices can have wide fluctuations and have been going down for the past several years.

Gold and silver numismatic (rare) coins are bought and sold for their intrinsic value and the public's demand for them. The main drawback to numismatic coins is overgrading. For example, when a dealer sells a rare coin, it might be graded MS (Mint State)–65. However, when the purchaser sells the same coin, far too many times it is downgraded to less than MS–65. This results in a big loss to the person who sells the coin.

But it goes beyond that, however, since coin dealers may cite a survey that rare coins were the best investment during a certain period. Often, these surveys are skewed by selecting only those coins that have appreciated the most. Most rare coins appreciate much less, and many even depreciate in value. Gold and silver investments are much to risky for the prudent investor.

LIMITED PARTNERSHIPS

Limited partnerships are like open-end mutual funds in that several people pool their money for investment purposes. While mutual funds invest primarily in stocks and bonds, limited partnerships may involve art, equipment leasing, real estate, oil and gas, and other types of investments.

In the1980s, limited partnerships were popular as tax shelters and income-producing investments. Now that the tax laws have changed, limited partnerships have less appeal. Some weaker partnerships are being combined into new ones called master partnerships, but even those are not appealing.

The advantages of limited partnerships are that any loss is limited to your investment (if this can be called an advantage), and any earnings are usually paid directly to you without being taxed at the corporate level.

The drawbacks to limited partnerships include the problem of evaluating their worth as good investments, high commission charges, and difficulty in reselling them. Limited partnerships can be risky and unattractive investments.

RENTAL REAL ESTATE

Today, rental real estate is no longer the "can't lose" investment that it was for so many years. The Tax Reform Act of 1986 ended most of the tax advantages of owing real estate other than your home.

The benefits of owning rental real estate are the possibility that it could increase in value and the leverage in financing it. However, at times, rental properties can be difficult to sell at the asking price. In addition, the maintenance and repair of properties may cause you irritation, considerable expense, and a large outlay of your time. Before you invest in rental real estate, you should ensure that rentals are in demand where you live, prospects are good for the property to increase in value, and you invest for the long term. Usually, there are better places than rental real estate to invest.

REAL ESTATE INVESTMENT TRUSTS

In addition to rental real estate, there are real estate investment trusts (REITs) in which you can avoid the management responsibilities of rental properties. The typical trust may own a portfolio of shopping centers, office buildings, or apartments. It is similar to owning real estate directly, but more liquid. Like stock mutual funds, REITs sell shares to the public to raise money, but instead of investing in stocks, they develop, own, and manage real estate. You can buy shares in a REIT the same way you'd buy shares of a stock. Before you invest in one, you should be certain that the trust has a strong cash flow, good earnings per share growth from year to year, a high yield, and experienced management.

UNIT INVESTMENT TRUSTS

Unit investment trusts (UITs), like mutual funds, invest in stocks or bonds with the pooled money received from investors. A UIT's value fluctuates with the value of its investments, just like a mutual fund.

While mutual fund managers often sell the investments in their portfolio, a UIT has no manager and their investments seldom change. Instead of a manager, a UIT has a board of directors who decide which investments to buy and they may be held until the trust matures, usually from a few months to five years. At maturity, investors can roll over their trust into a new one.

The advantages to UITs are that you know exactly what stocks or bonds are in the portfolio and there is no manager constantly buying and selling securities, which creates capital gains and losses that must be reported to the Internal Revenue Service (IRS).

The disadvantages to UITs are that their shares cannot be bought and sold each day. This makes it difficult to find out what the value of a trust is until it matures. Another disadvantage is that UITs usually have a sales charge.

CORPORATE BONDS

Most corporate bonds are sold as unsecured debentures backed by the corporation that issued the bonds. They are usually issued in denominations of $1,000 and their market price is listed daily in most large newspapers. Since the interest paid by the bonds is fixed their price will fluctuate, reflecting prevailing interest rates.

The main advantage of corporate bonds is that they pay a higher interest rate than government securities and they are sold in denominations as low as $1,000.

Their disadvantages are that corporate bonds may be redeemed by the issuer before they mature and the bondholder will no longer receive interest on the bonds; they fluctuate in price and if they are sold before maturity the bondholder could receive less than the price paid for them; corporations may default by not paying the interest and principal on their bonds; and the bonds are not backed by the federal government.

MUNICIPAL BONDS

Municipal bonds, or tax-exempt bonds as they are often called, are issued by state and local governments. Most are general obligation bonds, with interest paid by the taxing power of the issuer, or revenue bonds, with interest paid from a specific project such as a toll bridge or road.

Whether the tax-exempt feature of a municipal bond is more favorable than a taxable bond depends on your income tax bracket and the yield of the bond. To determine whether a taxable or nontaxable bond provides the higher yield, determine your tax bracket and subtract it from one hundred, and divide the tax-exempt yield by the result. The percentage is equal to a taxable yield. For example, if your tax bracket is 28 percent, a 5 percent tax-exempt yield is equal to a 6.94 percent taxable yield.

The main advantage of municipal bonds is their tax-free status. Their disadvantages are that some municipal bonds lack marketability because many are issued by small communities and not actively traded; there is a lack of information on them to determine their risk; and they usually come in denominations of $25,000 and up.

ZERO-COUPON BONDS

Zero-coupon bonds are debt obligations of a corporation, municipality, or the federal government. They are issued at a discount from their face value which is $1,000. For example, you might pay $300 for a $1,000 for a bond that yields 12 percent and matures in twenty years. The interest on zero-coupon bonds is compounded and paid in a lump sum when they mature. Even though interest is not paid until maturity, the IRS requires that the owners of zero-coupon bonds pay taxes on the interest earned each year as if it were actually received.

The advantages of investing in zero-coupon bonds are that a relatively high rate of interest is earned if they are held to maturity, they can be readily traded in the secondary bond market, and you know exactly what your investment will be worth at some point in the future, which makes long-term planning easier.

The drawbacks to zero-coupon bonds are that they can be subject to wide price fluctuations; their yield is set at a fixed rate until maturity, which could be unfavorable to the bondholder should interest rates rise; and they can be called in by the issuer before maturity.

BOND MUTUAL FUNDS

An investor in a bond fund essentially holds IOUs or promissory notes that pay interest at a fixed rate. In contrast, an investor in a stock fund is the part owner of a company and shares in possible earnings growth and the payment of dividends.

If you plan to buy government securities, or corporate, municipal, and zero-coupon bonds, consider a no-load bond fund. Despite their tendency to change in price as interest rates fluctuate, bond funds appeal to many investors as a medium-risk, income-type investment.

You'll find that a bond fund is less risky than owning an individual bond because a fund holds many bonds and, should one default, the remaining bonds would probably be secure. If you own an individual bond and it defaults, you could lose all your investment.

If you invest in a bond fund, here are some points to remember:

* Bonds fluctuate in price as interest rates rise and fall, and you may have an emergency situation that requires you to sell your fund when its price is at its lowest.

* Generally, bond funds don't provide as high a total return as stock mutual funds or common stocks.

* The fixed rate of return on a bond fund is a drawback in times of rapid inflation.

* Check several bond funds for one that charges a low rate for investing your money.

* Select a fund that holds at least BBB bonds as rated by Standard and Poor's or Baa bonds as rated by Moody's . The higher the rating, the more secure the bonds. For example, AAA bonds are more secure than BBB bonds.

* Avoid bonds with mortgage-backed securities.

COMMON STOCKS

Many people feel that investing in common stocks is too risky. To them, a passbook savings account, CD, or money market deposit account provides greater stability. It's true that the price of many stocks can be volatile at times, but it's also true that when you invest in quality stocks, you could be greatly rewarded.

There are two good reasons for buying stocks: They provide capital gains should their go up, and many pay dividends. What's more, some stocks that pay dividends have a dividend reinvestment program (DRIP). In this program, you can reinvest all or a portion of the dividends you receive to purchase additional shares of the company's stock, sometimes at a reduced market price and no commission. Of course, dividends that are reinvested can be withdrawn at any time.

Determining which are the quality stocks is not a time-consuming or difficult process. It involves developing some stock selection criteria and disciplining yourself to stick with them. With selection criteria, you increase your chance of buying quality stocks.

Not everyone should invest in stocks. The volatility of the stock market can be too stressful for some people. However, if you can handle the fluctuations of the market, you can include stocks in your investment plan.

MONEY MARKET MUTUAL FUNDS

No matter what your experience in financial matters, there is always a need to have some assets that you can quickly convert to cash. A money market mutual fund can fill that need.

Money market mutual funds can be taxable or tax-free. The taxable funds invest in short-term money market instruments such as commercial paper, CDs, treasury bills, and bankers' acceptances (used to finance international commercial transactions), while the tax-free funds invest primarily in the short-term maturing bonds of states and municipalities.

MMMFs are especially attractive because of the services they provide to their shareholders. These services include reinvestment of dividends, check-writing privileges, recordkeeping, and the opportunity to transfer money from one fund to another.

Although they are not insured, MMMFs are one of the safest investments available and pay a relatively high yield that varies with interest rates in general. In addition to the safety feature, the funds are liquid, which means that you can easily convert shares into cash with the use of a check-writing privilege. What's more, because most of the securities held by MMMFs are of large denominations, the small investor receives the same yield as the large investor.

Since all MMMFs invest in essentially the same type of securities, differences in their yield is a result of their expenses. Thus, the funds with the lowest expenses will usually have the highest yield.

There are three types of MMMFs, all of which invest in short-term debt:

* General purpose money market funds. General purpose funds invest in corporate debt, which accounts for most of their assets.

* Government money market funds. These funds invest in treasury securities and obligations from federal agencies. With this type of MMMF, you're not taxed at the state level on dividends received from the fund.

    *   Tax-exempt money market funds. Tax-exempt funds invest in primarily state and local municipal securities. The interest earned by these funds is free from federal taxes and may be tax-free at the state level.

GROWTH MUTUAL FUNDS

Growth mutual funds are open-end investment companies, which means there is no limit on the number of shares the fund can issue. Growth funds are the ones you should rely on to power your investment portfolio to double-digit returns.

Basically, growth funds invest in the common stock of companies that are expected to increase in market value at an accelerated rate or provide above-average dividend income. Although all growth funds invest in equities, some specialize in fast-growing companies, while others look for undervalued companies.

One thing to remember is that growth funds fluctuate in price as economic conditions adjust from cycles of prosperity and recession. Thus, any drop in the price of a fund during a decline may take years for you to get even. For this reason, fund shares that you purchase during a market decline will prove to be more profitable than those you purchase near a market top. That means to stay fully invested in your fund throughout market cycles. In Chapter 6, you'll learn how to take advantage of market cycles by using Dollar-Cost Averaging Plus to invest in growth funds.

Because of the desirable features of growth funds, it's a good idea to consider them as the main holding in your investment plan. Later on, as you gain experience and confidence, you can diversify into individual stocks and other types of investments.

SUMMING UP

The list of investment choices does not include every way your money can be put to work. It covers only those investments that are readily available and those with ample information about their past performance.

It's to your advantage to stick primarily with sound and secure investments such as money market mutual funds, growth funds, bond funds, and quality common stocks. These investments are easy to buy and sell, and information on them is always available.

It's usually best to avoid investments such as gold and silver, limited partnerships, unit trusts, rental real estate, and bank instruments, such as CDs, whose true value is eroded by inflation.

When you invest, the preservation of your capital should be your main concern. To preserve your capital, keep away from investments that carry a lot of risk and those that can't keep up with inflation, and you should come out ahead.

CHAPTER 3
BASIS OF MUTUAL FUNDS

There are two general types of mutual funds: closed-end and open-end. Closed-end funds have a fixed number of shares and usually trade on one of the stock exchanges. Open-end funds, the more popular of the two types, have an unlimited number of shares and are not listed on an exchange. This book covers only open-end funds, since they usually provide shareholders a greater investment return than closed-end funds.

An open-end mutual fund is a company that pools money from shareholders and invests it in securities such as stocks, bonds, and cash equivalents. The number of securities in a fund may range from as few as twenty-five to fifty, to as many as a few hundred. When you buy shares in an open-end fund, you own a portion of the securities held in the fund. As the securities move up or down, the price of your fund changes accordingly.

TYPES OF OPEN-END MUTUAL FUNDS

Since there are so many open-end mutual funds, it is difficult to classify them by type or investment objective. For example, a stock fund with an objective to invest in small growth companies may also hold shares in medium-sized growth companies. Another fund's objective may be to provide its shareholders with maximum dividend income but hold shares in companies that pay relatively low dividends. Probably

31

the best classifications of open-end mutual funds are the ones assigned by the Investment Company Institute in its **Directory of Mutual Funds:**

Aggressive growth funds "seek maximum capital gains as their investment objective. Current income is not a significant factor. Some may invest in stocks of businesses that are somewhat out of the mainstream, such as fledgling companies, new industries, companies fallen on hard times, or industries temporarily out of favor. Some may also use specialized investment techniques such as option writing or short-term trading."

Balanced funds "generally have a three-part investment objective: to conserve the investor's initial principal, to pay current income, and to promote a long-term growth of both principal and income."

Convertible securities funds "invest in debt securities that can be converted into equity securities of the issuing corporation."

Corporate bond funds, "like income funds, seek a high level of income. They do so by buying bonds of corporations for the majority of the fund's portfolio. The rest of the portfolio may be in U.S. Treasury bonds or bonds issued by a federal agency."

Flexible portfolio funds "may be 100 percent invested in stocks or bonds or money market instruments, depending on market conditions. These funds give the money managers the greatest flexibility in anticipating or responding to economic changes."

Funds of funds "invest in other mutual funds under the premise that the additional layer of diversification further reduces investment risk."

GNMA or Ginnie Mae funds " invest in mortgage securities backed by the Government National Mortgage Association (GNMA). To qualify for this category, the majority of the portfolio must always be invested in mortgage-backed securities."

Global bond funds "invest in the debt securities of companies and countries worldwide, including the U.S."

Global equity funds "invest in securities traded worldwide, including the U.S. Compared to direct investments, global funds offer investors an easy avenue to investing abroad. The funds' professional money managers handle the trading and recordkeeping details and deal with differences in currencies, languages, time zones, laws and regulations, and business customs and practices. In addition, to another layer of diversification, global funds add another layer of risk—exchange-rate risk."

Growth funds "invest primarily in the common stock of well-established companies. Their primary aim is to produce an increase in the value of their investments (capital gains) rather than a flow of dividends. Investors who buy a growth fund are more interested in seeing the fund's share price rise than receiving income from dividends."

Growth and income funds "invest mainly in the common stock of companies that have had increasing share value but also a solid record of paying dividends. This type of fund attempts to combine long-term capital growth with a steady stream of income."

High-yielding bond funds "maintain at least two-thirds of their portfolios in lower rated corporate bonds (Baa or lower by Moody's rating service and BBB by Standard and Poor's rating service). In return for a generally higher yield, investors must bear a greater degree of risk than for higher-rated bonds."

Income (bond) funds "seek a high level of current income for their shareholders by investing at all times in a mix of corporate and government bonds."

Income (equity) funds "seek a high level of current income for their shareholders by investing primarily in equity securities of companies with good dividend-paying records."

Income (mixed) funds "seek a high level of current income for their shareholders by investing in income-producing securities, including both equity and debt instruments."

Index funds "construct portfolios to mirror specific market indexes. These funds are expected to provide a rate of return over time that will approximate or match, but not exceed, that of the markets they mirror."

International funds "invest in equity securities of companies located outside the U.S. Two-thirds of their portfolios must be so invested at all times to be categorized here."

Long-term municipal bond funds "invest in bonds issued by states and municipalities to finance schools, highways, hospitals, airports, bridges, water and sewer works, and other public projects. In most cases, income earned on these securities is not taxed by the federal government, but may be taxed under state and local laws. For some tax payers, portions of income earned on these securities may be subject to the federal alternative minimum tax."

Long-term state municipal bond funds "work just like other long-term municipal bond funds (see above) except their portfolios contain the issues of only one state. A resident of that state has the advantage of receiving income free of both federal and state tax. For some taxpayers, portions of income from these securities may be subject to the federal alternative tax.

Money market mutual funds "invest in the short-term securities sold in the money market. These are generally the safest, most stable securities available, including treasury bills, certificates of deposit of large banks, and commercial paper (the short-term IOUs of large U.S. corporations)."

Precious metals/gold funds "maintain two-thirds of their portfolios invested in securities associated with gold, silver, and other precious metals."

Short-term municipal bond funds "invest in municipal securities with relatively short maturities. These are also known as tax-exempt money market funds. For some taxpayers, portions of income from these securities may be subject to the federal alternative minimum tax."

Short-term state municipal bond funds "work just like other short-term municipal bond funds (see above) except their portfolios contain the issues of only one state. A resident of that state has the advantage of receiving income free of both federal and state tax. For some taxpayers, portions of income from these securities may be subject to the federal alternative minimum tax."

Small company funds "typically seek growth of capital by investing primarily in equity securities of relatively small companies. Small companies are usually defined in terms of their market capitalization, generally less than $1.5 billion. Shares of these companies often trade in over-the-counter markets and may be relatively thinly traded. Such shares may be subject to more abrupt and erratic market movement than those of large corporations or the stock market in general."

U.S. government income funds "invest in a variety of government securities. These include U.S. Treasury bonds, federally guaranteed mortgage-backed securities, and other government notes."

Additional Information

You can request a copy of the **Directory of Mutual Funds** from the Investment Company Institute, 1401 H Street NW, Washington, DC 20005-2148, telephone number 202-293-7700, or through their website at www.ici.org.

FUND PROSPECTUS

A mutual fund cannot sell you shares without giving you a prospectus, the official document that describes a fund and its policies. A prospectus should provide enough information so you can decide if you want to invest in a fund. It's a good idea to check more than one prospectus so you will select a fund that meets your investment objectives. Here's a rundown on the most important items to check in a prospectus.

Objective

In the prospectus, all funds specify their investment objective. For example, an objective could be long-term growth of capital, high level of current income, or some other investment goal. The objective can range from low-risk and high-return investments to high-risk and low-return investments. Make certain that the fund's objective is compatible with your reasons for investing in it.

Annual Operating Expenses

Annual operating expenses   usually consist of two charges: management fees and other expenses. The operating expenses of most funds are between 0.75 percent and 1.75 percent of net assets.

In addition to operating expenses, some funds have front-end loads, 12b-1 fees, or back-end loads. These charges are described in more detail in Chapter five.

Other Information

The Securities and Exchange Commission (SEC) recommends that a mutual fund prospectus follow a basic format and most funds comply with the recommendation. A prospectus usually includes the following information:

* The fund's performance since it began operations.
* How to purchase shares.
* How to redeem shares.
* Minimum investment requirement.
* The fund's management.
* Dividend and capital gains distributions.
* Portfolio turnover.
* Dividend reinvestment plan.
* Automatic monthly investment plan.
* Shareholder rights.
* How to convert to another fund.
* Check-writing privileges.
* Income tax advise.
* Special services, such as telephone exchange of shares.

A prospectus can be difficult to read. And it doesn't tell you how the fund performed in comparison to similar funds. You can get that information by reading a fund newsletter, or by requesting a prospectus from several funds and then making a comparison.

MANAGEMENT OF FUNDS

Although a mutual fund is essentially owned by its shareholders, a board of directors is responsible for administering the fund's investment policy, including the selection of the fund's manager. The manager is usually paid a fee based on the fund's total assets to handle the securities in the fund. A transfer agent, usually a bank, maintains records for the fund's shareholders.

NET ASSET VALUE

The net asset value (NAV) is the price of a fund's shares. The NAV is calculated each business day by subtracting liabilities from the value of securities held in the fund and dividing by the number of shares outstanding.

INITIAL INVESTMENT MINIMUM

The minimum initial investment to open an account is set by each fund. A few funds have no minimum, and others require as much as several hundred dollars. However, most set their minimum between $500 and $2,500. The minimum for later investments is much lower than the initial investment minimum, usually from $50 to $100. The minimum to open an IRA is usually less than the minimum for a regular investment, on average about $250.

FUND DISTRIBUTIONS

When you buy shares in a mutual fund, you must decide whether to reinvest any dividends and capital gains distributions paid by the fund. Most shareholders reinvest their distributions to buy additional shares in the fund, rather than receiving them in cash.

Since mutual funds register with the SEC as regulated investment companies, they do not pay taxes if they distribute their investment dividends and most capital gains to their shareholders. They merely serve as conduits for distributions to pass from the fund to their shareholders. Except for some municipal bond funds, all distributions you receive are taxable, and you must report them to the IRS.

LEGISLATION OF FUNDS

Federal and state laws regulate the activities of mutual funds. These laws require the disclosure of fund operations to the SEC, state regulators, and their shareholders. Four federal laws regulate mutual funds:

* Securities Act of 1933. This law requires that all mutual funds file a registration statement and provide information to the SEC. It also directs funds to provide current and potential investors with a prospectus that contains information on the fund's management, objectives, and policy.

* Securities Exchange Act of 1934. This act makes funds liable to antifraud provisions and regulations by the SEC, and the National Association of Securities Dealers.

* Investment Advisors Act of 1940. This legislation regulates the actions of investment advisors to mutual funds.

* Investment Company Act of 1940. This act contains provisions to prevent conflicts of interest and self-dealing in the management of funds.

RECORDKEEPING AND REPORTING

Most mutual funds maintain good records for their shareholders. Each time you make an investment, redeem shares, or receive a distribution, you receive a confirmation that contains the following:

* Date of the transaction.

* Dollar amount of the transaction.

* Price at which shares were bought or sold.

* Number of shares bought or sold.

* Total shares held in your account.

You'll always get quarterly or semiannual reports as well as a yearly report from your fund. These reports show the securities held by the fund, the fund's performance during the reporting period, and other financial information.

At the end of each year, you will receive a Form1099-DIV that shows all distributions paid to you by the fund. The 1099 form separates dividends and capital gains distributions. This division is useful since you can offset capital gains against capital losses for tax purposes.

CHAPTER 4
MUTUAL FUNDS—ADVANTAGES AND DISADVANTAGES

Mutual funds offer something for all kinds of investors. Some investors buy them for their security; others for their services. Many find them attractive to save for the down payment on a house, college expenses for the children, or supplementing retirement.

There are three ways to make money in mutual funds: through dividends and interest earned by a fund's investments; when the securities held by a fund are sold at a profit; and by any increase in the value of the securities held by a fund.

There is no guarantee that a fund will provide you with a generous return, yet the return on many funds has been very good. Usually, the longer your investment period, the greater your return.

Keep in mind that there are disadvantages to mutual funds, but they are surpassed by the advantages that funds offer. Let's look at their advantages.

ADVANTAGES OF MUTUAL FUNDS

Professional Management

Mutual fund managers are full-time, experienced professionals. Most of them have a good investment strategy that many individual investors may lack. For this reason, many managers attract investors to their particular funds.

Since they have a large amount of money to invest, fund managers can get the latest information about securities, which may be difficult for the small investor to obtain. Managers usually base their investment decisions on factors such as the growth potential of particular industries, earnings outlook for individual securities, and general economic conditions. Few individual investors can match the experience and skill of fund managers.

Diversification

Diversification is an investment principle that requires holding more than one type of security to reduce risk. To diversify their portfolios, mutual fund managers invest in securities such as common stocks, bonds, and money market instruments.

When you invest in a fund, you automatically own a portion of several securities, a diversified portfolio. When the price of a fund goes down, some of its securities may drop substantially in price, while others may drop only slightly or even increase in price.

One type of fund is not highly diversified. This is the specialty or sector fund which invests in a specific industry such as utilities, health care, or technology. However, this type of fund still diversifies within the specific industry.

There is also an unfavorable side to diversification. A fund may invest in so many different securities that its performance only matches the market indexes. All types of securities move in cycles, and the ideal approach is for a fund to catch the right one on the upswing, whether it is a group of stocks or an industry. What works best is the right diversification at a particular time.

Regulation

Federal and state laws tightly regulate what mutual funds can and cannot do with their investors' money. These laws require that funds disclose their operations to the SEC and other regulatory authorities. In addition, funds must furnish their shareholders with periodic statements that disclose their current securities and latest investment results.

Convenience

It's easy and convenient to invest in a mutual fund. You can handle the paperwork to open an account and make later investments from your home. The fund takes care of the bookkeeping and provides you with an account statement after each of your transactions.

To open an account, all you do is telephone the investment company that handles the fund and ask for a prospectus, which is free of charge. Then, if the prospectus meets your investment requirements, complete the application and return it to the fund. Most funds maintain toll-free telephone lines in case you have any questions about the prospectus.

If you feel that you need help to select a fund, then you can buy funds through a broker, bank, or financial planner. In that case, however, you will probably be advised to invest in a load fund that reduce the amount of money you receive when shares are sold.

Low Initial Investment

Some funds require no minimum initial investment. However, many do have a minimum that is usually within the budget of most investors. The relatively low minimum proves helpful to people who have a limited amount to invest at one time.

Competitive Investment Return

Compared to other investments, many mutual funds have provided a very good return on investors' money. If you are willing to take reasonable risks and put some of your money in growth funds, you should be able to earn a double-digit return over the long term, ten years or more.

Ease of Monitoring

It's easy to monitor the progress of your fund. The financial section of most large newspapers provides a list of all of the funds. Newspapers such as **Investor's Business Daily** and **The Wall Street Journal** not only list all of the mutual funds but also provide detailed data and other helpful information on funds.

Shareholder Services

Mutual funds provide many services to their shareholders, and they continue to provide better services each year. The list of the services that funds provide include the following:

* Voluntary savings. No-load funds are voluntary as opposed to load funds that charge a commission and may require periodic investments. In a no-load fund, you can make your initial investment and purchase additional shares at any time without charge.

* Automatic monthly investment plan. Once you open an account with a fund, you may authorize your bank to make regular payments from your checking or savings account to your fund. Most banks will honor automatic transfer of funds, but you should check with your bank first to ensure that it has this service. In addition, your employer may have a payroll deduction plan that will automatically deduct money from your salary and send it to your fund.

* Automatic reinvestment of distributions. If you choose, you can reinvest all or part of the dividends and capital gains distributions paid by a fund to buy additional shares. This is done through a fund's automatic reinvestment plan (ARP). An ARP is a good idea not only because it gives you the opportunity to acquire more shares but also because it prevents you spending the distributions if you receive them in cash. There is no minimum investment requirement when you reinvest your distributions.

The reinvestment of distributions is a means of forced savings that incorporates the principle of dollar-cost averaging, a method of investing at regular intervals. The idea is that you will purchase more shares when the price of a fund is low and fewer shares when it is high.

* Conversion privileges. Many funds are part of a family of funds that usually includes stock, bond, and money market funds. Some families even include international, global, specialty, sector, and commodity funds. If your fund is part of a family, you usually can switch from one fund to another within the family. Since your investment goals may change through the years, the privilege to switch funds is an important service. For tax purposes, the exchange of one fund for another is treated as a sale and must be reported to the IRS for the year the exchange is made.

* Systematic withdrawal plans. Many funds have a withdrawal plan that will allow you to receive payments at regular intervals. You can receive payments from dividends, capital gains, or sell some of your fund's shares on a monthly, quarterly, or yearly basis. However, most funds require a minimum balance of $5,000 to participate in the plan.

* Liquidity. You can cash in all or part of your shares in a fund at any time and receive their current market value, which may be more or less than your original cost. Most funds will redeem shares upon a written or telephone request. However, when the redemption exceeds a specific amount, many funds require a signature guarantee.

* Recordkeeping. Most mutual funds keep good records for their shareholders. When you make an investment, redeem shares, or switch from one fund to another, you will receive a confirmation of the transaction from the fund. Depending on the fund's policy, you will also receive an update of your account on a quarterly, semiannual, or yearly basis.

* Ease of investing. Once you open an account, there are usually three convenient ways to invest in your fund. You may transfer money to your fund from your bank or your place of employment, invest by telephone or wire, or mail payments to your fund.

DISADVANTAGES OF MUTUAL FUNDS

Although mutual funds have a lot to offer, they still have their disadvantages, the biggest of which is the high cost of investing in funds. This is seen in load funds that have front-end loads, 12b-1 fees, or back-end loads.

A fund's performance can be another drawback. Some funds consistently earn an above-average return; others perform poorly. The idea is to select a fund that, through the years, has consistently provided a good return.

A final criticism of mutual funds is the handling of capital gains. If you own a fund that pays capital gains, taxes must be paid on the gains for the year you receive them. If you own an individual stock, you pay no capital gains tax until the stock is sold.

CHAPTER 5
SELECTING A MUTUAL FUND

With so many mutual funds to choose from, you may wonder how to select one that's right for you. It's not as difficult as it may seem. The first step is to take another look at your investment goals. Next, decide on the amount of investment risk you can handle. And then, develop some criteria to select a fund.

MATCH YOUR INVESTMENT GOALS WITH YOUR RISK LEVEL

Before you select a mutual fund, reexamine your investment goals. Your goals will help to determine the type of fund to invest in. For example, if you want to invest to supplement your retirement, which is over five years away, consider a growth or index fund. But if you are within five years of retirement and will need extra income, a growth and income may be best.

Next, decide on the investment risk you feel comfortable with. Do you have a low-, medium-, or high-risk level when you invest? If you worry a lot about your investments, then you probably have a low risk level. On the other hand, if you are the type of person who can handle the price fluctuations of the more volatile funds, you probably have a high-risk level.

If risk doesn't bother you, consider either an aggressive growth fund or a growth fund. If you can handle only a medium amount of risk, think about a growth and income fund. If you want to play it safe with low risk and moderate investment income, consider a U.S. government income fund.

After you decide your investment goals and your risk level, match them with a fund's objective. To do that, review Chapter 3 and select the type of fund with the objective that meets your requirements. The idea is to match your investment goals with the objective of a fund at the level of risk you feel comfortable with. Once you identify the type of fund that meets your investment requirements, set up selection criteria to screen the available funds.

SELECTION CRITERIA

Few people would buy a house without first looking at several and then selecting the one that best meets their needs. You should select a mutual fund the same way. Thus, it's a good idea to set up selection criteria to help you screen the available funds. The most important criteria are performance, cost, and services. If a fund rates high on all three, consider it for your investment plan.

Performance

Before you buy shares in a mutual fund, you should review its past performance—its track record, the fund's total return compared to other funds and the market indexes. Although the past performance of a fund is not always an indication of its future results, it is still a good measure to use when you select a fund. It's better to consider only those funds that have been good performers for several years. You'll find that some funds perform well for a year or so, but have a poor overall record.

What is the best way to determine a fund's performance? You measure its annualized return against an index that is indicative of the stock market. Since stock market indexes assess the up and down price movements in their component stocks, you can use them as a yardstick for measuring a fund's performance. There are several market indexes, but the three most widely used are the Dow-Jones Industrial Average, Standard and Poor's 500 Index, and the NASDAQ (National Association of Security Dealers Automated Quotation System) Composite Index.

The Dow-Jones Industrial Average of thirty stocks, probably the best known of all the indexes, measures general stock market price movements. The Dow-Jones is called an average rather than an index because no adjustment is made in the number of shares outstanding in its component stocks.   Some complaints have been directed at the Dow-Jones. One is that it samples too small a percentage of the stocks listed on the New York Stock Exchange. Although the sample includes about 25 percent of the total value of all stocks on the exchange, it is still small. Another complaint is that the Dow-Jones contains too many cyclical stocks and under-represents growth stocks. Nevertheless, the Dow-Jones Industrial Average is the main index most people use when referring to the stock market. Still, the Dow-Jones will rarely be an appropriate benchmark to measure your mutual fund's performance because it tracks only 30 large U.S. companies.

The Standard and Poor's (S&P) 500 is the index most mutual fund managers use to measure their fund's performance. Within the S&P 500 are over four hundred industrial, forty utilities, and twenty transportation stocks. This index includes stocks that represent over 75 percent of the market value of all those on the New York Stock Exchange.

The NASDAQ Composite Index is a computerized price reporting system that covers more than two thousand over-the-counter (OTC) stocks. This index includes industrial, bank, insurance, finance, transportation, and utility stocks.

If you measure a fund's performance against an index, be certain to use the appropriate one. For example, if a fund holds stocks that are listed on the New York and NASDAQ exchanges, use the S&P 500 to measure its performance. Use the NASDAQ Composite for a fund that invests primarily in OTC stocks, and the Dow-Jones averages when a fund invests mainly in stocks on the Dow-Jones. When you compare a fund's performance to a market index, be sure to consider the reinvestment of dividends and capital gains that the fund pays.

And remember, superior returns do not guarantee the future success of a fund.

When you compare funds, make sure you are comparing funds that have not only the same investment objectives, but also the same investing style. Thus, if you are considering a growth fund that invests mainly in undervalued growth companies, compare its results against other growth funds using the same style.

Cost

You can invest in a mutual fund without the use of a full-service broker, insurance agent, or financial adviser—who mainly sell front-end load funds. You can deal directly with a no-load fund and thus avoid all commissions.

To further reduce your expenses, you can invest in a fund that has no back-end load or 12b-1 fees. The following are all the fees that a fund can impose. It's a good idea to become familiar with these fees before you invest in a fund.

* Management and customer service fees. You must pay fees to the investment company for the management and services that a fund provides. Since both load and no-load funds have these fees, they cannot be avoided. In a fund's prospectus, the fees are listed as a percentage of the fund's net assets and usually total 0.75 percent to 1.75 percent.

* Front-end load. Front-end load is a sales charge or commission ranging from 1.0 percent to 8.5 percent that a load fund deducts from each investment. For example, if your initial investment is $1,000 and the sales commission is 8.5 percent, your actual investment is only $915. What's more, the fund levies the commission on later investments and the reinvestment of distributions. Over several years, commissions amount to a lot of money—money that is deducted from your investment with no benefit to you.

* Back-end load. Some funds assess a charge when you redeem shares, called a back-end load. It can amount to about 4 percent

up to 8 percent of the value of the redemption. Funds that don't have front end-loads often assess back-end loads as a way to hide their commissions.

* 12b-1 fee. A 12b-1 fee is also known as a hidden load. The original intent of the fee was to aid funds with their marketing and distribution expenses. However, its original purpose may have changed to gouge the naive investor. The 12b-1 fee can reduce your investment in a fund by as much as 2 percent to 3 percent.

Here's an illustration of how fees can affect your investments in a fund. Let's take a hypothetical situation and assume that you make a lump-sum investment of $1,000 in an 8.5 percent load fund that has a 12b-1 fee of 1 percent, service charge of 1 percent, and redemption fee of 4 percent. We'll further assume that you sell the fund after one year, with no change in its price.

Cost of your initial investment (8.5 percent of $1,000)	$85
12b-1 fee (1 percent of $1,000)	$10
Management and customer service fee (1 percent of $1,000)	$10
Redemption charge (4 percent of $895)	$36
Total charges	$141
Amount you receive at redemption	$859
Percent of loss on your investment	14.1 %

An investment of $1,000 for one year in this hypothetical fund has charges of $141. Compare this to a pure no-load fund—a fund with no front-end load, back-end load, or 12b-1 fee—that charges only $10 for management and service fees. In addition, there is no clear evidence that load funds per se outperform no-load funds.

When you invest in a fund, there is no valid reason to pay a front-end load, back-end load, or 12b-1 fee. Read a fund's prospectus carefully, and if there are fees other than a management and customer service charge, reject it.

Services

The third selection item to consider is the services a fund offers its shareholders. If you follow the suggestions in this book, you will consider only no-load funds. You'll find that these funds provide convenient and reliable services to their shareholders, and there are no high-pressure sales tactics by their representatives.

No-load funds provide many services that you can access by mail, telephone, or website. You can open an account with a fund, add shares to the account, and usually sell all or part of the shares you own in a fund. Make certain before you open an account that a fund provides all of the services that you want.

OTHER SELECTION CRITERIA

Besides performance, cost, and services, here are some other criteria to consider when you select a fund.

Management changes

A fund's performance is closely tied to its management. Thus, it's a good idea to note any recent changes in the top management of a fund. A change in management does not mean that a fund will perform better or worse than before the change. What it does mean is that a new manager may have a new investment style or philosophy that is different from yours.

If the manager who is responsible for a fund's investments is no longer with the fund, you should be careful about using past performance as a predictor of a fund's future performance. The effect of a manager change can vary widely on how the fund is managed, and the fund's future return. What all good managers have in common, however, is the ability to accurately assess the future prospects of individual companies.

Business Week's yearly Mutual Fund Scorecard shows whether the current manager has held the job for at least ten years. This publication as well as the fund itself will give you an indication about the tenure of a fund's manager.

In addition to management changes, you should be comfortable with the investment philosophy of the fund's manager. Find out how a manager picks stocks, whether the manager tries to balance the fund or invests a large percentage of the fund's assets in only a few stocks, if the manager invests in the fund, and what determines how much cash the fund holds.

Risk

All investments, including mutual funds, involve risk. It's much easier to assess risk when you invest in gold, commodities, and limited partnerships than in many mutual funds.

Sometimes those funds that perform the best over the long term are the ones that are willing to take added risk by investing in more speculative stocks. Looking at the past performance of a fund, covering several years, is more important than trying to determine a fund's risk.

Some financial publications use betas to determine a fund's risk. A beta usually measures a fund's volatility to that of the S&P 500 Index over a period of years. For example, if a fund's beta is 1.00 it should move in line with the S&P. A fund with a beta of 1.60 is 60 percent more volatile than the S&P Index and is presumably more risky.

Although betas provide some indication of risk, they should not be given too much weight when you consider a fund. As a rule, a fund's past performance is a more important selection factor than its beta.

Turnover ratio

Turnover ratio is the yearly rate at which a fund buys and sells securities in its portfolio. A high turnover rate is not evidence that a fund's performance will be good or poor. Often, a high turnover rate may indicate that the fund's manager is rotating investments into stock groups that show promise of increasing in value and out of those that are decreasing. In market advances, stock leadership changes from one industry group to another and fund managers may sell lagging groups and buy advancing ones. Other managers may sell those stocks whose balance sheets or price movement charts are turning negative and buy those which look more promising.

One effect of a high turnover rate is that fund expenses increase. These consist of brokerage commissions and the bid/ask price spreads for buying and selling stocks. However, don't let a high turnover rate stop you from investing in a fund that meets your other selection criteria.

Tax-efficiency

Before you buy shares in a mutual fund, it's a good idea to check its tax-efficiency—a measure of your return after you pay taxes on a fund's dividend and capital gains distributions. A fund with 100 percent tax-efficiency means you have no tax liability on the distributions.

Many fund managers pay little attention to taxes, but every time a manager sells a stock above its cost it constitutes a capital gains. Thus, a manager who sells a winning stock to lock in profits also saddles the fund's shareholders with a tax bill. The more trading a manager does, of course, the more likely it is that the fund will pay capital gains, unless the manager can offset gains with losses.

Except for mutual funds held in a retirement account, a fund's payment of distributions to its shareholders must be reported to the IRS. Thus, an indication that you will be subject to taxes is the fund's turnover rate.

Not only does a high turnover rate result in an increase in a fund's expenses, but it also can reduce the fund's assets. A reduction in a fund's assets combined with an increase in fund redemptions can change a winning fund into a losing fund. Remember, a good fund manager strives for high profits, and focuses on your after-tax return—a figure usually not mentioned in the fund's prospectus.

Size of Fund

With few exceptions, large funds are seldom the top performers in a rising market and seldom the worst performers in a falling market. In most cases, the size of a fund is something to consider but nothing to worry about. What amount of assets makes a fund large? The figure is arbitrary, depending on whose yardstick you use. However, for our purposes, funds with assets over $1 billion will be considered large.

The larger funds, because of their huge assets, usually invest in companies that have many shares outstanding. Thus, they may miss the opportunity to invest in smaller companies with fewer shares and greater growth potential. There is no doubt that small funds can be more flexible with their investment decisions since they can buy shares in relatively small companies that can be good performers in a rising market.

In some cases, when a fund grows too large, management will start a new fund with the same investment objective. The cloning of the original fund provides greater flexibility, and the new fund may show a greater percentage increase in price than the larger fund.

If you invest in a large fund and find that its performance is less than its peer funds, then you should be concerned. Whatever the reason for the poor performance, you should consider switching to another fund.

New Funds

Although it's best to base your selection of a fund on the performance, cost, and services of established funds, there may be times when you want to invest in a new fund. Since new funds have no investment record on which to judge their performance, it's usually better to avoid them.

However, there is an exception to investing in new funds. When an investment company that manages existing funds that are good performers offers a new fund, it presumably could perform as well as the existing funds that the investment company manages.

Buying Shares

There are four ways to buy shares in a mutual fund: through a brokerage house, insurance company, financial adviser, or directly from the fund. When you buy a pure no-load fund, you can deal directly with the fund and you pay no sales commission. Why pay a broker, insurance agent, or financial adviser a 1.0 percent to 8.5 percent commission for something that you can do yourself?

To buy shares in a no-load fund, all that's required is that you call or write the fund for a free prospectus. If the prospectus meets your selection criteria, fill out the enclosed application and mail it to the fund with a check to cover your initial investment.

Since a prospectus is usually in legal-type language, it can be difficult to understand. If you have any questions, contact the fund and request a "statement of additional information" which has more details on the prospectus.

In addition to dealing directly with a fund, you can contact a discount broker. Many of these firms handle several no-load funds for a small fee.

PURE NO-LOAD FUNDS

The following two lists include many no-load funds—funds that have no front-end load, back-end load, or 12b-1 fee. The first list contains growth funds and the second one income funds. The lists are a good starting point for the selection of a fund. For a free copy of a fund's prospectus, call the telephone number on the right side of the list.

SELECTED GROWTH FUNDS
WITH NO FRONT-END LOAD, 12b-1 FEE,
OR BACK-END LOAD

Fund	Ten-Year Annualized Total Return*	800 Telephone Number
American Century Growth	8.9	345-2021
American Century Heritage	9.8	345-2021
Barron Asset	12.2	992-2766

Dreyfus Founders Discovery	12.1	896-8238
Fidelity Contrafund	13.8	343-3548
Fidelity Mid-Cap Stock	14.8	343-3548
Fremont U.S. Micro-Cap	19.8	548-4539
Gabelli Growth AAA	10.4	422-3554
Janus Venture	11.3	525-3713
Scudder Small Cap Growth	12.8	621-1048
T. Rowe Price Mid-Cap Growth	16.1	638-5660
T. Rowe Price New Horizons	13.5	638-5660
Turner Small Cap Growth	15.8	224-6312
Value Line Emerging Opportunities	15.1	243-2729
Value line Special Situations	14.3	243-2729
Vanguard Explorer Inv.	12.5	851-4999
Vanguard Growth Inv.	11.6	851-4999
Wasatch Ultra Growth	15.5	551-1700

* Note: Includes change in net asset value and reinvestment of distributions for the period ending December 31, 2004.

SELECTED INCOME FUNDS
WITH NO FRONT-END LOAD, 12b-1 FEE,
OR BACK-END LOAD

Fund	Five-Year Annualized Total Return*	800 Telephone Number
American Century Strategic Allocation; Conservative	5.0	345-2021

Fidelity Asset Manager: Income	5.2	343-3548
Fidelity Freedom Income	4.1	343-3548
Russell Conservative Strategy	4.8	787-7354
T. Rowe Price Personal Strategy Income	6.5	638-5660
Vanguard Wellesley Income	8.9	851-4999

* Note: Includes change in net asset value and reinvestment of distributions for the period ending December 31, 2004.

FAMILY OF FUNDS

Many mutual funds are part of a larger grouping called a family of funds. The individual funds within the family have different portfolio managers but are under the direction of the same investment company. A family may include stock, bond, treasury, international, and money market funds. When you select a fund that belongs to a family, you can usually switch to another fund within the family. The opportunity to switch funds is useful since your investment objectives may change through the years. In addition, you could maintain a money market fund for emergency purposes within the family.

Here's a table of pure no-load fund families that have growth, growth and income, and money market funds. You can obtain a free prospectus on any of these funds by calling the telephone number in the table.

SELECTED NO-LOAD FUND FAMILIES
WITH GROWTH, GROWTH/ INCOME, AND
MONEY MARKET FUNDS

Fund family	800 Telephone Number
————————	————————
American Century–20th Century	345-2021
Fidelity	343-3548
Janus	525-3713

Neuberger & Berman	877-9700
Scudder	621-1048
Strong	368-6860
T. Rowe Price	638-5660
Vanguard	851-4999

TOTAL RETURN TEST

If you want to know the past performance of a fund, you can use a total return test. It's easy to use, and you can apply it to any fund. The total return of a fund stems from dividends and capital gains paid plus the change in the fund's price. When you combine these three items, you can compute a fund's total return or yield. Here's an illustration of how to determine a fund's total return.

Total Return Test
XYZ Fund

Category	Amount
—————	—————
Dividends paid per share	$ 0.40
Capital gains distributions per share	$ 2.10
Subtotal	$ 2.50
Fund price at end of year	$24.00
Fund price at beginning of year	$20.00
	—————
Subtotal gain (loss) in fund price	$ 4.00
Totals:	
Total return	$ 6.50 ($2.50 plus $4.00)
Total return percent	32.5 percent ($6.50 divided by $20.00)

Once you determine a fund's total return, you can compare it to the return on other funds or the market indexes. Remember, even the best of funds may experience years when total return will not outperform the market indexes. However, the better funds will have more up than down years, and this is where to confine your selection.

INFORMATION SOURCES

Where can you find the information you need to select a fund? The place to begin is to ask for a prospectus from the fund that interests you. Since a fund's prospectus contains its historical performance according to a standard format, it's easy to compare different funds. How do you get a prospectus? You can receive a prospectus by calling the fund and asking for one. Many libraries carry the addresses and telephone numbers of mutual funds.

In addition, there are several publications that provide information on mutual funds. Here are some of them and what they cover.

Standard and Poor's Stock Guide furnishes statistical information on several hundred funds. This guide, issued monthly, contains a section on mutual funds. It includes the type of fund, such as growth, bond, income; the fund's total assets; high/low price per share for the last five years; minimum investment required; sales fees; the increase or decrease in value of an assumed $10,000 investment for funds during the last five years; and much more.

Investor's Business Daily contains a section on mutual funds. In each issue, this newspaper includes mutual fund performance rankings; percent of price change in the current year; current price; whether the fund is load or no-load; type of fund, and feature articles on funds.

Other sources of information include **Forbes, Barron's,** *Money,* and **Business Week,** which once a year rank funds according to their performance, risk, and other factors. Also, **Morningstar's Mutual Fund Values,** and **Weisenberger's Investment Companies** issue information on funds.

WEB SITES

There are several Web sites that provide information on mutual funds. These sites maintain a large data base so you can compare a fund's performance, holdings, and return. Here's a list of Web sites that can help you select a fund:

Brill's Mutual Funds Interactive www.fundsinteractive.com

FundAlarm www.fundalarm.com

IndexFunds.com www.indexfunds.com

Morningstar www.morningstar.com

Quicken.com www.quicken.com

CHAPTER 6
DOLLAR-COST AVERAGING PLUS

Successful investing in mutual funds is more a skill than a science. Success rests on examining several funds for investment, selecting the fund that promises the best return on your money, and considering new investment strategies for investing in the fund you select.

Dollar-Cost Averaging Plus (DCAP) is a new strategy for investing in mutual funds. DCAP is not a "get rich quick" scheme; rather, it is a long-term investment formula. It functions on the belief that the general trend of most mutual fund prices is up, and that within this trend, funds will experience both up and down price volatility. The DCAP formula requires that you increase investments when fund prices are relatively low and level off investments when their prices are high. One attractive feature of the formula is that it relieves you of trying to decide when is the best time to invest in funds.

It requires little time and effort to apply the DCAP formula, and you don't have to be an expert on financial matters or mutual funds to use it. DCAP does not guarantee that you won't have losses, yet it could provide you with an above-average return on mutual funds.

Although the formula is an investment strategy that works best with mutual funds, you can also use it to buy individual shares of stock. Whether you use the formula to buy shares in funds or stocks, it can help you build that nest egg for college, provide a down payment on a house, supplement your retirement, or attain some other goal.

DEVELOPING THE DCAP FORMULA

There are many ways to invest in mutual funds. For example, typical dollar-cost averaging and lump-sum payment are two of the more popular ones. The DCAP formula is an effective refinement of the typical and often used strategy of dollar-cost averaging.

Several investment methods were tried before the DCAP formula began to take shape. As the formula evolved, issues had to be decided before it could be put to use.

The first issue was the selection of a fund. The DCAP formula provided a higher return when one of the better performing funds was selected. In addition, an even greater return was realized with a fund that had a wide high/low price range.

Since the formula required a target price to control the amount of each investment, it was important to set it as accurately as possible. After testing several methods, it became evident that it was best to set the target price in relation to the high/low price range of the fund. Also, it made little difference whether the target price was set to the fund's price range for a three-, five-, or ten-year period. This is simply because those funds that were good performers provided an above-average return almost every year.

Another issue was how much monthly investments should be increased if a fund's price dropped below the target price. This was resolved by correlating the amount of each investment to a maximum 25 percent drop allowed in a fund's price before investments stopped. Therefore, each 5 percent decrease in a fund's price below the target price required that investments be increased 20 percent to a maximum of 100 percent. As a rule, when the price of the better performing funds dropped below the target price, this usually created a buying opportunity.

The final issue concerned the reasons for ending investments should a fund drop sharply in price. Four reasons caused a fund to drop steeply in price: The fund had poor management, there was a change in the fund's management, the fund's investment strategy changed, or general economic conditions badly deteriorated. When any of these occurred with a 25 percent drop in a fund's price, it was better to switch to another fund or invest temporarily in a money market fund.

DCAP VS. TYPICAL DOLLAR-COST AVERAGING

The typical method of dollar-cost averaging has been around for a long time and is one of the easiest ways to invest in mutual funds. It consists of investing a fixed amount of money in a fund at regular intervals. When you invest a fixed amount, fewer shares are bought when the fund is relatively high and more shares when it is low. The advantage of this method of investing is that the actual cost per share is usually less than the average price paid during the investment period.

In comparison, DCAP is a refinement of the typical method of dollar-cost averaging. The typical method requires that the amount you invest, whether at monthly, yearly, or other intervals, remains the same. DCAP requires that you invest monthly, and the amount of each investment varies in relation to a target price.

DCAP is an investment formula based on the assumption that the general trend of most mutual fund prices is up, but there will be both up and down price fluctuations in their rise. To take advantage of these fluctuations, DCAP requires that you set a target price to control the amount of your monthly investments. If your fund's price per share, its net asset value (NAV), drops below the target price, you increase the amount of your monthly investment. However, if your fund's price is higher than the target price, the amount of your investment stays the same.

In many ways DCAP is similar to typical dollar-cost averaging, but there are differences:

* With the DCAP formula, investments are monthly, while typical dollar-cost averaging requires investments monthly, quarterly, yearly, or at other intervals.

* The amount of DCAP investments can vary, while the amount

of typical dollar-cost averaging investments remain constant.

* DCAP requires the setting and resetting of a target price that determines the amount of each investment. Typical dollar-cost averaging does not require a target price.

COMPARISON OF DCAP WITH DOLLAR-COST AVERAGING

Any new investment strategy should prove that it is better than existing ways of investing. To see how the DCAP formula compares with typical dollar-cost averaging, let's invest in two imaginary funds.

We'll name the funds XYZ and XYZ-T. Both funds are the same except for one variable. Investments in XYZ Fund are according to the DCAP formula, and investments in XYZ-T Fund are consistent with typical dollar-cost averaging. XYZ-T has no target price, but XYZ has a $20 target price. Thus, if XYZ's price drops below the target price the amount of the monthly investment increases.

When you compare the funds, note that the XYZ Fund using the DCAP formula provides a higher rate of return than typical dollar-cost averaging. The DCAP return is 15.6 percent, and the typical dollar-cost averaging return is 13.4 percent, a difference of 2.2 percent. A difference of 2.2 percent becomes a significant amount when you compound it for several years.

The initial investment in each fund was $500. Later investments in the XYZ Fund were in relation to the DCAP formula's target price and ranged from $100 to $180 a month. Investments in XYZ-T Fund were held constant at $100 a month.

DOLLAR-COST AVERAGING PLUS XYZ FUND

Date of Investment	Dollar Amount of Investment	Cost Per Share	Number of shares Bought	Total Shares
01-01-05	$500*	$20	25.000	25.000
02-01-05	$100	$21	4.761	29.761

03-01-05	$100	$22	4.545	34.306
04-01-05	$100	$20	5.000	39.306
05-01-05	$120	$19	6.315	45.621
06-01-05	$140	$18	7.777	53.398
07-01-05	$160	$17	9.411	62.809
08-01-05	$180	$16	11.250	74.059
09-01-05	$160	$17	9.411	83.470
10-01-05	$100	$20	5.000	88.470
11-01-05	$100	$21	4.761	93.231
12-01-05	$100	$22	4.545	97.776

Value of XYZ Fund on 12-01-05 $2,151
Dollar amount invested $1,860
Dollar amount gain (loss) $291
Rate of return   15.6 percent
    * Initial investment
    Note: Table excludes capital gains and dividends

TYPICAL DOLLAR-COST AVERAGING XYZ-T FUND

Date of Investment	Dollar Amount of Investment	Cost Per Share	Number of Shares Bought	Total Shares
01-01-05	$500*	$20	25.000	25.000
02-01-05	$100	$21	4.761	29.761
03-01-05	$100	$22	4.545	34.306
04-01-05	$100	$20	5.000	39.306
05-01-05	$100	$19	5.263	44.569
06-01-05	$100	$18	5.555	50.124
07-01-05	$100	$17	5.882	56.006
08-01-05	$100	$16	6.250	62.256
09-01-05	$100	$17	5.882	68.138
10-01-05	$100	$20	5.000	73.138

| 11–01-05 | $100 | $21 | 4.761 | 77.899 |
| 12-01-05 | $100 | $22 | 4.545 | 82.444 |

Value of XYZ-M Fund on 12-01-05	$1,814
Dollar amount invested	$1,600
Dollar amount gain (loss)	$214
Rate of return	13.4 percent

   * Initial investment

Note: Table excludes capital gains and dividends

The minimum monthly investment could be higher or lower than $100. If the minimum is $50, for example, the rate of return for both funds would be the same. The rate of return is what's important when comparing the two funds, not the amount you invest each month.

Remember, both funds are hypothetical and contain arbitrary figures, so there is no guarantee that you can earn a 15.6 percent return on your investment. Still, if you review the return on many funds, a 15.6 percent or even higher is possible.

DCAP'S COMPONENTS

When you invest according to the DCAP formula, there are four components to consider: initial investment, target price, amount of monthly investment, and maximum investment amount. To see how the formula's components function, let's look at this hypothetical investment.

Assume that you decide to invest in XYZ Growth Fund because it holds quality growth stocks, seems well-managed, and shows an average annual total return of 16 percent for the last five years. Moreover, after you satisfy the fund's initial investment requirement of $1,000, you decide to invest a minimum of $100 each month. Here's a rundown of DCAP's components and how they function in relation to your hypothetical fund.

Initial Investment

Your initial investment of $1,000 at $20 per share buys 50.000 shares in XYZ Fund. (The number of shares in mutual fund transactions are carried to three decimal places which accounts for fractional ownership of shares.)

Target Price

To set the target price, let's assume that for the last five years the trading range of XYZ Fund was from a high of $22 to a low of $17, and its current price is $20. Since you feel that $20 is a fair price for the fund, you set that figure as your target price.

Monthly Investment Amount

As long as the price of XYZ Fund stays above the $20 target price, your monthly investment will be $100. Your investments will exceed $100 only if XYZ's price drops below the $20 target price.

The table below lists the amount of your monthly investments in relation to changes in the price of XYZ Fund. The table provides an easy way to determine the amount of your investments. Later in this chapter, there is a detailed example under the heading "How the DCAP Formula Works."

MONTHLY INVESTMENT TABLE XYZ GROWTH FUND

Target Price	Fund's Price Per Share	Percent of Fund's Price Increase or Decrease from Target Price	Dollar Amount of Monthly Investment
$20	$20	0	$100
$20	$19	-5	$120
$20	$18	-10	$140
$20	$17	-15	$160
$20	$16	-20	$180
$20	$15	-25	$200

$20	$16	-20	$180
$20	$17	-15	$160
$20	$18	-10	$140
$20	$19	-5	$120
$20	$20	0	$100
$20	$20	0	$100

All figures in the monthly investment table are rounded to the nearest dollar for simplicity. For example, if XYZ's price per share is $19.50, it is rounded down to $19 as the basis for your monthly investment. Similarly, if the price is $19.51, it is rounded up to $20.

In the table, the amount of your investment varies in relation to the change in XYZ's price from the target price. During the investment period, the target price remains at $20. If you feel that the target price is set too high or too low, reset it using one of the other methods explained later in this chapter.

The minimum monthly investment in the table is $100. If you decide to set your minimum at $50, divide the last column in the monthly investment table by two, and the result is the amount of your investment. For example, if the fund's price is $17, a 15 percent drop from your target price, your monthly investment is $80. The main idea of the DCAP formula is the percent of increase or decrease of each investment, not the amount you decide to use as a base.

Maximum Investment Amount

There is a limit to your investments when XYZ Fund drops in price. Thus, each 5 percent drop in XYZ's price below the target price requires that you increase your monthly investment 20 percent, but only to a maximum of 100 percent. A 100 percent increase in your monthly investments correlates to a 25 percent drop in XYZ's price, and that great a decrease could indicate the fund has a problem.

THE TARGET PRICE

The target price determines the amount of your monthly investments. It is a trigger mechanism that rises or falls in relation to your fund's price. When accurately set, it could greatly increase the value of your investment in a fund.

To illustrate the function of the target price, let's suppose that you make an initial investment of $1,000 in a fund at $20 per share and plan to invest a minimum of $100 each month. Further, let's assume you feel that the fund's price of $20 is a good target price to determine the amount of your future investments.

If the price of your fund drops to $19 (a 5 percent decrease), you increase the amount of your monthly investment by 20 percent, to $120. Similarly, if the price drops to $18 (a 10 percent decrease from the target price), you increase your monthly investment 40 percent, to $140. Thus, every 5 percent drop below the target price requires a 20 percent increase in your investment, to a total of 100 percent. If the price then rises from $18 to $20, the target price, your monthly investment would decrease from $140 to $100.

The base or minimum amount of the monthly investment used in this illustration is $100. Naturally, your base amount could be greater or less than $100. The amount should be what you can afford and still meet the minimum requirements of the fund.

SETTING THE TARGET PRICE

After you open an account with a fund, but before your first monthly investment, set the target price. There are various methods you can use to determine where to set the target price. Here's a rundown on the best methods to use.

Current Fund Price

You may set the target price at your cost per share when you open your account with a fund. In this case, if your initial investment cost is $20, your target price is $20, and monthly investments are in relation to the $20 target price. When you use your initial cost per share as the target price, you assume the fund is fairly valued at that price.

Median Price of Fund

Another way is to set the target price in relation to the high and low price range of your fund for the past year or multiple of years. For example, if the high/low range of your fund for the previous year was from $20 to $16, set the target price at $18, the median price. Similarly, if the range was from $20 to $14, set the target price at $17, again the median price.

Using the median price for a five- to ten-year period instead of for one year should give you a more accurate account of a fund's volatility, presumably in both up and down market cycles. To illustrate, let's say a fund's high/low range was from $24 to $16 for the past five years, the period you select to set the target price. In this case, set the target price at $20. All monthly investments in your fund are in relation to that price.

Market Indexes

Several indexes measure the stock market's performance. Three of the most widely used are the Dow-Jones Industrial Average, Standard and Poor's 500, and NASDAQ Composite Index. Suppose that you select the Dow-Jones Industrial Average for the past year to determine where to set your target price. If the Dow-Jones is 20 percent below its high for the past year, set your target price 20 percent below the fund's high price for the past year. Similarly, if you use the S&P 500, or the NASDAQ, set the target price the same percentage as the index is below its high.

Before you select a market index, look at your fund's prospectus or quarterly reports and note which exchange lists most of the fund's stocks. Then select that exchange to set the target price. For example, if most of your fund's stocks are listed on the NASDAQ, choose the NASDAQ to set the target price.

There are several ways to set your fund's target price and none of them is flawless. They are merely methods you can use to determine the amount of your monthly investments. Of the methods discussed, probably the more accurate one is the median price of your fund for the past few years. This assumes that your fund has been in operation for the period you select.

HOW THE DCAP FORMULA WORKS

Now that you are familiar with DCAP's components, let's look at the actual DCAP formula. To make the formula easy to apply, these alpha designations are used:

A = target price

B = fund price

C = target price less fund price

D = 20 percent variance multiplier

E = monthly investment increase

F = monthly investment base amount

G = total monthly investment

DCAP formula: A - B = (C x D) = (E + F) = G

The following is an example of how the DCAP formula works. In the example, the fund's trading range is $22 to $18. the target price is $20, and the minimum monthly investment is $100.

In the example of the DCAP formula, the target remains at $20 during the 12-month investment period. When the fund's price is below the target price, the difference is multiplied by a 20 percent variance to arrive at the increase or decrease in the amount of your monthly investment.

Any increase in your monthly investment is added to the minimum monthly investment of $100 to determine your total investment. The minimum monthly investment could be higher or lower than $100 and the formula would not change.

Before each investment, compare your fund's price to the target price to determine the amount of your investment. You can get your fund's latest price from most large newspapers, the library, or by calling your fund.

DCAP FORMULA

A Target Price	− B Fund Price	= Target Price Less Fund Price	(C Times 20 Percent Variance	x D) Monthly Investment Increase	= (E Monthly Investment Base Amount	+ F) Total Monthly Investment	= G
$20.00	$20.00	0	.20	0	$100	$100	
$20.00	$18.55	$1.45	.20	$29	$100	$129	
$20.00	$18.09	$1.91	.20	$38	$100	$138	
$20.00	$17.52	$2.48	.20	$49	$100	$149	
$20.00	$17.20	$2.80	.20	$56	$100	$156	
$20.00	$16.94	$3.06	.20	$61	$100	$161	
$20.00	$17.44	$2.56	.20	$51	$100	$151	
$20.00	$18.28	$1.72	.20	$34	$100	$134	
$20.00	$18.72	$1.28	.20	$26	$100	$126	
$20.00	$19.50	$0.50	.20	$10	$100	$110	
$20.00	$20.00	0	.20	0	$100	$100	
$20.00	$22.09	0	.20	0	$100	$100	

RESETTING THE TARGET PRICE

There is good advice in the saying "if it works, don't fix it." You can apply the same reasoning to your fund's target price. There are only three reasons for you to reset the target price: when you set it in relation to the high/low price of your fund and your fund sets a new high price; when you set it in relation to one of the market indexes such as the Dow-Jones, Standard & Poor's, or the NASDAQ and the index sets a new high price; and when your fund makes a distribution. If you plan to invest in your fund for the long term, say 10 to 15 years, you may have to reset the target price only a few times during that period.

Resetting the Target Price for New Highs

If you set the target price in relation to the fund's price and it sets a new high, the target price is reset. For example, let's suppose you invest in a fund with a price range from $24 to $20 and you set the target price at $22. Then the fund rises to a new high of $25. In this case, reset the target price at $22.50, the medium price. You can apply the same methodology when you use the Dow-Jones, S&P 500, or the NASDAQ Index as a reference to set the target price.

The target price is reset when your fund sets a new high price but not for a new low price, unless the new low occurs after a distribution, which is explained below. In case of a new low, monthly investments increase to a maximum of 100 percent from the target price, but the target price is not reset.

Resetting the Target Price for Distributions

There are two ways to receive distributions from your mutual fund—dividends and capital gains. When you receive distributions, the fund provides you with a statement that shows the date and dollar amount of the distribution, number of new shares purchased (if you reinvest your distributions in the fund), purchase price of the new shares, and the total shares you own. You can use the statement to help you determine if your fund's target price needs to be reset.

When a fund makes a distribution, the price of a fund is adjusted downward to reflect its new value. For example, if a fund's price is $21 the day before a distribution of $0.50, its price will decrease to $20.50 after the distribution. Because the securities held by the fund may increase or decrease in value the day of the distribution, they also must figure into the new price of the fund.

Taking the example a step further, suppose the securities held by the fund fell $0.50 on the distribution date. In that case, the new price of the fund is $20. You arrive at the $20 by deducting $0.50 for the distribution and $0.50 for the decrease in the securities held by the fund.

Let's look at the above example again and assume that the fund's trading range is $23 to $16 before the distribution, and the target price is $20. Since the price of the fund did not drop below the $20 target price on the distribution date, the target price is not reset.

Only when a distribution, with an increase or decrease in a fund's price, changes the trading range is the target price reset. When you reset the target price after a distribution, usually it is to a lower figure and may require an increase in your monthly investments.

Let's take a situation where the price of your fund is $20, the trading range is from $21 to $19, and the target price is $20. Your fund then declares a $1.50 distribution, and on the distribution day the fund drops $0.50 in value. In this situation, the new trading range is $21 to $18 and the new target price is $19.50. this would require an increase of $30 to a $100 minimum monthly investment.

Determining the Target Price for New Low after Distributions

Here's an example of how to determine the target price and amount to invest when your fund sets a new low after a distribution.

Pre-distribution:

Trading range of fund	$ 21.00 to $ 19.00
Price of fund	$ 20.00
Target price	$ 20.00
Amount of monthly investment	$100.00
Amount of distribution	$ 1.50
Increase or decrease in fund price on distribution	$ 0.50

Post-distribution:

Trading range of fund	$ 21.00 to $ 18.00

($1.50 + $0.50 = $2 deducted from
pre-distribution price of $20)

Price of fund ($20 less $2)	$ 18.00
Target price	$ 19.50
(median price of new trading range)	
Amount of monthly investment	$130.00

(new target price of $19.50 less
new fund price of $18.00 = $1.50 x
20 percent variance = $130.00)

Determining the Target Price for New High after Distributions

Only rarely will a fund set a new high price on the day of a distribution. Should a new high occur on that day, reset the target price to reflect the fund's new trading range.

For example, let's imagine that a fund's trading range is $20 to $18, the target price is set at $19, and the current price of the fund is $19.50. The fund pays a distribution of $0.25 and rises $1 on the same date. In this situation, the fund set a new high at $20.25, and the new target price is $19.62. The new target price is determined by adding the $1 increase in the fund's price to $19.50 and deducting the $0.25 distribution. Then the fund's high price ($20.25) and low price ($18) are added and divided by two to arrive at $19.62.

The initial setting and then resetting of the target price is the key to greater profits when you use the DCAP formula. Be sure to examine the target price before each monthly investment, after distributions, and when your fund sets a new high.

CHECKING YOUR FUND'S PERFORMANCE

As you would take your car in for an inspection or tune-up, you should periodically check your fund's performance. After you invest in your fund for about a year, check its total return. Total return measures your fund's performance based on the change in its share price and distributions.

To compute an approximate return, take the number of shares you own and multiply them by the current price of the fund. That will give you the market value of your shares. Next, add up the amount of your investments and subtract the total from the value of your shares. This will show whether your investment has increased or decreased in value.

You can divide the dollar amount of the increase or decrease by the amount of your investments to determine the percent of return. Here's an illustration of how to figure your fund's total return. Let's say your fund is $20 at the beginning of the year and $22 when the year ends. During the year, it paid $0.80 a share in dividends and $1.60 a share in capital gains.

Price of fund at beginning of year	$20.00
Price of fund at end of year	$22.00
Increase in value of fund	$ 2.00
Dividends paid	$ .80
Capital gains paid	$ 1.60
Total return	$ 4.40
Total return rate ($4.40 divided by $20)	22 percent

To determine your fund's performance in relation to the market indexes, you can compare its total return to that of the Dow-Jones Industrial Average, S&P 500 Index, or the NASDAQ Index for the same period.

You will receive reports from your fund that show its return compared to one or more of the market indexes, usually the S&P 500. If your fund consistently underperforms the indexes, you should consider selling it. There is no reason to continue investing in a fund that doesn't regularly outperform the market indexes.

DCAP RESERVE FUND

It's a good idea to have a DCAP reserve fund in addition to your mutual fund. The reason for the reserve fund is to have money available to increase investments in your mutual fund when required by the

DCAP formula. What's more a reserve fund can serve as your emergency fund. If your mutual fund is part of a fund family, a money market fund is usually available to use as your reserve fund.

When you invest by the DCAP formula, monthly investments stop if your fund drops 25 percent in price. Should this occur, a reserve fund is a convenient place to invest the money that has been destined for your fund. The idea here is to keep in the habit of investing monthly. Later, when you decide whether to continue to invest in the same fund or switch to another, you can reinvest the money.

CHAPTER 7
INVESTMENT GUIDELINES

Before you invest, set some guidelines. The most successful investors are those who have guidelines to follow. Besides helping you reach your goals, guidelines also give you the emotional satisfaction of knowing that you have put your financial plan to practical use.

Many newsletters and financial publications are ready to give you investment advice, usually at a fee. Some of the advice is good, but much is poor. When you have guidelines, it's much easier to determine which is the good advice and to make informed investment decisions. Here are some guidelines to consider before you invest.

SET INVESTMENT GOALS

Determine your goals before you make any investment decision. Do you want to build a nest egg for your children's education? To provide for the down payment on a house? To supplement your retirement income?

Your goals should affect all your financial decisions, from the amount and type of your insurance policies to your investment selections. When you set goals, you take charge of your financial future.

DEVELOP AN INVESTMENT PLAN

It's hard to achieve your goals unless you have an investment plan. A plan will provide direction when you invest and force you to take charge of your finances. It will add continuity to your financial affairs which is better than acting automatically, hoping everything will be all right.

SELECT INVESTMENTS THAT SUIT YOUR GOALS

The best investments for your portfolio depend on your investment goals and time frames. Investments with low risk are more appropriate for short-term goals such as saving for the down payment on a house in a few years. For long-term goals like saving for retirement, you should select growth investments and be less concerned about their short-term price fluctuations.

HAVE AN EMERGENCY FUND

Before you invest, set aside about three months of your net income in a money market mutual fund or bank account for unexpected emergencies. There is no good reason to hold investments if you have to sell them to pay for an emergency.

BEFORE YOU INVEST CHECK YOUR INSURANCE PROGRAM

It's to your advantage to have adequate life, health, accident, disability, and mortgage insurance before you invest. The amount of insurance you need depends on your age, the number and age of your dependents, and your health.

DEBT MANAGEMENT

If you have debt, don't invest until it's under control. It makes no sense to start an investment program when you have excessive debt. If you use over 20 percent of your net income for charge and credit card payments, you may have too much debt.

UNDERSTAND INVESTMENT BASICS

To prudently manage your investments, you should understand the basics of investing in mutual funds, stocks, bonds, government securities, and real estate. When you understand investment basics, you increase your prospects for a good return on your investments.

DON'T TAKE UNNECESSARY RISKS

Risk is the chance that you will lose all or part of your investment money. If you want a guarantee that you won't lose any money, invest in government securities, savings accounts, insured bonds, and insured money market mutual funds. However, if you invest in those securities, you run the risk that your investment return will be less than the rate of inflation. To earn a good return, one that will outpace inflation, you should assume a reasonable amount of risk in investments such as mutual funds, stocks, bonds, and real estate.

BUILD YOUR INVESTMENT PORTFOLIO GRADUALLY

Whether you have a large amount or only a few hundred dollars to invest, it's usually better to move slowly. This requires investing bit by bit rather than all of your money at one time. For example, if you plan to invest $2,000 in a mutual fund, invest the money in increments of $500 a few weeks apart.

DIVERSIFY YOUR INVESTMENT PORTFOLIO

A diversified portfolio holds more than one investment. For instance, you could invest in mutual funds, stocks, bonds, and a money market fund. With a diversified portfolio, you lessen your risk should one type of investment not prove profitable. The right balance for your portfolio will depend on your age, your risk tolerance, and the investment goals you've set.

DON'T HAVE MORE INVESTMENTS THAN YOU CAN MONITOR

If you over-diversify your portfolio, you may have so many investments that you can't follow all of them. A portfolio that holds too many investments can be as risky as one that has only a few investments.

MANAGE YOUR OWN PORTFOLIO

If feasible, you should manage your own investment portfolio. Managing your portfolio, means you'll need to know the basics of investing in the various financial markets. When you understand the basics, you'll have more confidence in your investment decisions.

As your own manager, don't ignore the counsel of others. There may be times when you will need the services of an accountant, insurance agent, or financial planner.

DON'T HOLD TOO MUCH IN CASH

If you want to keep up with inflation, invest most of your money in mutual funds, stocks, and real estate. The return on cash investments such as savings and checking accounts offer little chance to outpace rising prices.

USE MUTUAL FUNDS FOR YOUR PORTFOLIO'S FOUNDATION

Mutual funds have many advantages that other investments don't offer. Funds are easy to buy and sell, provide quality investor services, and many have earned double-digit returns. Because of these advantages, funds are ideal investments as the foundation of your portfolio. Once the foundation is built, you can diversify into other investments.

BUY ONLY TOP PERFORMING NO-LOAD MUTUAL FUNDS

Which are the top performing no-load mutual funds? Chapter 5, "Selecting a Mutual Fund," answers that question. Keep in mind that some funds consistently do better than others. A fund's good performance record is not a guarantee that it will perform well in the future. Yet it's a good starting point for selecting a fund.

INVEST IN MUTUAL FUNDS FOR THE LONG TERM

When you invest in a mutual fund, consider it a long-term investment. The big gains in mutual funds usually are made by those who use a buy and hold strategy.

A few investors are fortunate enough to time their investments, being in a fund when its price is rising and selling before it drops. This involves the strategy of market timing that is not only difficult but also risky.

INVEST MONTHLY IN YOUR MUTUAL FUND

Mutual funds are especially attractive to people who want to invest each month. Moreover, if you invest all your money at one time, you could pay too high a price for a fund. Monthly investments using the DCAP formula may provide a greater return on your money than one-time or sporadic investments in a fund. Investing monthly has another very good aspect—it gets you in the habit of saving.

REINVEST MUTUAL FUND DISTRIBUTIONS

Mutual funds offer automatic reinvestment plans in which you can have dividend and capital gain distributions put back in the fund to purchase additional shares. The reinvestment of distributions, a form of dollar-cost averaging, is a good way to increase your return on a fund.

AVOID EXCESSIVE FUND SWITCHING

It's usually not wise to use conversion privileges to switch in and out of funds randomly. Most studies show that trying to time the rise and fall of different funds is not as profitable as staying with one fund. The opportunity to switch funds is a useful service, but you should use it with discrimination.

AVOID STEEP LOSSES ON MUTUAL FUNDS

Owning treasury securities guarantees that you will receive interest on your investment and your principal will be repaid at maturity. Owning shares in a mutual fund has no guarantee, and there is always the chance that you will lose a large part of your investment. Although some funds carry more risk than others, you can adopt safeguards so you won't lose all your money.

The DCAP formula, for example, limits losses by putting a cap on the amount of money you invest in a fund. When you invest by the DCAP formula, you can never lose more than 25 percent of your investment. In addition, the setting and resetting of the DCAP target price will make you aware of any continuous and significant decline in the price of your fund.

You can expect a certain amount of up and down price movement with a fund, but one that drops in price and remains down for a long period may have problems. In this case, it's usually best to sell the fund.

BUY ONLY QUALITY STOCKS

Quality stocks can be found in almost every industry. These stocks are industry leaders with sales and earnings that increase almost every year. They usually offer products or services with growth potential, pay dividends, and emphasize the development of new products or services. Their management is usually aggressive and experienced. These are the companies to consider if you invest in stocks.

SET A LOSS LIMIT ON STOCKS

Before you invest in stocks, set a limit on the loss you will tolerate if they drop in price. If you buy a stock at $30, for example, limit any loss to 10 percent. In this case, you would sell the stock if it drops to $27. When you limit losses, most of your money is available to buy another stock that may prove profitable.

AVOID PRICE LIMIT ORDERS ON STOCKS

Seasoned investors rarely use price limit orders (the execution of an order at a specific price—or better) when they buy and sell stocks. Setting a limit order on a stock is a poor practice because you are quibbling for a small percentage point, rather than stressing the overall movement of a stock. With a limit order, you could completely miss a stock's move on the upside and not get out of a stock quick enough on the downside.

BE PATIENT WITH STOCKS

Guard against jumping in and out of the stock market. If you own a stock and feel that it will move up in price, have the patience to wait. Your chance to make a profit may come a few days after you sold the stock.

USE MARGIN WITH CARE

If you use margin (borrow money from a broker) to invest in mutual funds or stocks, use it sparingly. It's true that you could double your profits by using margin, but you could also double your losses. What's more, if you have a margin account and your investments drop in value, your broker may ask that you add money to your account.

If you have a margin account, it's important that you have some strict rules. Here are two rules for investing on margin: use margin only during an advancing stock market, and borrow less than the maximum allowed.

OPEN AN INDIVIDUAL RETIREMENT ACCOUNT (IRA), KEOGH PLAN, OR OTHER RETIREMENT PLAN

If you are eligible, contribute to a tax-deferred retirement plan. It's surprising how quickly tax-deferred investments can increase in value when compared to those that are taxable.

BE YOUR OWN RETIREMENT PLAN MANAGER

There is a shift underway in business and government that places more responsibility for retirement on the employee's shoulders. This is seen in the move from defined-benefit retirement plans, where the employer guarantees retirement benefits, to defined-contribution plans that put more responsibility for retirement on the employee. If you have a defined-contribution plan, you'll need to learn how you can best manage your plan.

UNDERSTAND YOUR RETIREMENT PLAN'S BENEFITS

If you have a retirement plan, it's only smart to understand its benefits. Find out the maximum you can contribute to your plan each year; your investment choices; if you can switch among investments; your vesting rights; date you are eligible for retirement; and the payout options of your plan.

DON'T INCLUDE TAX-FREE INVESTMENTS IN YOUR RETIREMENT PLAN

Since treasury securities, U.S. savings bonds, and municipal bonds are fully or partially tax-free, don't include them in your retirement plan. Tax-free investments may have a place in your portfolio, but there is no valid reason to include them in your retirement plan.

BE CAREFUL WITH INDIVIDUAL BONDS

If you buy municipal or corporate bonds, consider a bond fund. Buying individual bonds can be risky. When you invest in a bond fund, your risk is reduced because you own a part of several bonds as opposed to a single bond that could drop significantly in price or default on its interest payments.

DON"T INVEST ON TIPS, RUMORS, AND FANTASTIC PROMOTIONS

Since the first step in making money is not to lose it, don't listen to investment tips, rumors, and "too good to be true" promotions. This may be difficult advice to follow, yet investing on tips, rumors, and promotions is an easy way to lose your money.

Many investors who lose money in the financial markets invest in promotions based on newspaper advertisements, a telephone sales pitch, or a boiler room operation promising big profits. Investors who are victims to those frauds spend almost no time investigating the organization promoting the investment or the risks involved.

DON'T INVEST IN ANYTHING YOU DON'T UNDERSTAND

Whether you make your own investment decisions or rely on someone else, take time to learn about an investment.

AVOID INVESTMENTS IN GOLD, SILVER, ART, AND COLLECTIBLES

Investing in precious metals, art, and collectibles carry a large amount of risk. Many people tout them as a hedge against inflation, but other investments with less risk can provide the same hedge.

DON'T GET INVOLVED IN SELLING SHORT, OPTIONS, AND COMMODITIES

Selling short, options, and commodities investments are risky, so it's usually better to avoid them. Few people consistently make money with short selling, options, or commodities.

OWN YOUR OWN HOME

If you can afford it, own your home. Owning rather than renting gives you a financial advantage. When you pay rent you don't build up equity; when you own your home you do. When you rent none of your payments are tax deductible; when you own your home you get a deduction for real estate taxes and mortgage interest. Moreover, any profit from selling your home could be tax free.

BE AN INFORMED INVESTOR

You should follow your investments closely. With the large amount of financial publications available, you can easily obtain information about investments. Although knowledge doesn't guarantee success, it may help you make better investment decisions and avoid losses.

To become an informed investor, you should do more than occasionally read the financial pages in the local newspaper. You need to have an understanding of investment basics and the financial markets.

A good way to learn about mutual funds is to contact a fund and ask for a free prospectus. To learn about specific stocks, write for a company's annual report which is free of charge.

Other ways you can learn about investments include enrolling in an investment course at a local school and checking with the nearest library for information.

SUMMARY

It's to your advantage to set some guidelines before you invest. They don't have to be complex—just basic rules to follow. As you gain investment experience, you will probably add more guidelines to the above list. The important point is to have guidelines and stick with them.

CHAPTER 8
BUILDING YOUR PORTFOLIO

A portfolio is the total of all your salable items. This includes property such as mutual funds, stocks, bonds, real estate, art, bank accounts, and money market funds. For example, your portfolio may contain three mutual funds, two stocks, a bank account, money market fund, and the equity in your house, with a total value of $150,000.

Contrary to what some people think, there is nothing complex about building and managing your portfolio. If you follow the suggestions in this book, you can do it easily.

Before you allocate any money for new investments, look at your current investments. Are you satisfied with them? Do they carry too much risk for you? Do they provide a good return on your money? Once you decide this, match the return you expect and your risk level with available investments. This way you can shape a portfolio that you will feel comfortable with.

DIVERSIFICATION

All investments carry a degree of risk. One way to reduce risk is to diversify your portfolio by holding more than one type of investment. If you put all your money in one investment, you could suffer a big loss should something go wrong. Even if you have only a small amount of money to invest, allocate it among more than one investment to reduce risk.

When you invest in a growth mutual fund, you get immediate diversification. That's because a growth fund holds a variety of securities such as stocks, bonds, and cash equivalents. If you also invest in a money market fund, government securities, and a bond fund, your portfolio would be even more diversified and less risky.

Diversification does not mean investing in as many different types of securities as possible, but selecting a few that are not too risky and yet have the potential to provide a good return on your money.

SAFETY OF PRINCIPAL

When you build your investment portfolio, your first concern should be the safety of your principal—the protection of your original investment. Put another way, the first step to making money is not to lose it. Clearly, if you don't lose money, you've done nothing more than break even. That means you'll have to invest your money to come out ahead.

Not surprisingly, safety of principal is inconsistent with a good return on an investment. If you want a good return, you must take some risks and accept the likelihood you may lose some of your principal. You can usually protect your principal and earn a good return if you avoid highly speculative investments and those that you don't fully understand.

PORTFOLIO VARIABLES

You should consider some variables before you start your portfolio. Variables will determine the kinds of securities you should buy and how long you should hold them. Above all, variables will help determine the amount of risk you should accept.

The first variable is your age. Usually, the younger you are the more speculative investments you can hold in your portfolio. If you are close to retirement age your portfolio probably should be more conservative.

If you have many years until retirement, your portfolio could hold medium- to high-risk securities.

Another variable is your occupation. If your income is steadily increasing, your portfolio might contain more risky investments than that of someone whose income is uncertain.

The number of dependents in your family and the amount of your debt also should influence the way you shape your portfolio. A single person with no debts can usually hold more speculative investments than someone who has three children, car payments, and a house mortgage.

PORTFOLIO BUILDING BLOCKS

The building blocks for your portfolio could be mutual funds, stocks, and bonds. You can invest in them as your family's situation requires or as money becomes available. Deciding whether mutual funds, stocks, or bonds are best suited for you involves two questions: one is the risk level acceptable and; two, which kinds of investments are best to achieve your goals.

Stocks have the potential to provide the greatest return. They also offer the best chance for you to beat inflation. Bonds don't provide much protection against inflation because they pay a fixed return, but bonds prosper when the economy is weak. Mutual funds are less risky than stocks and can meet the needs of many investors.

There are two ways to build your portfolio—all at once or gradually. Most investors build their portfolios gradually, investing at regular intervals through the years. Building your portfolio should not be complicated. Yet, it will need monitoring and careful management, but not frequent changes.

How you build and manage your portfolio should depend on your investment time horizon, your risk level, tax implications, and changes in your investment goals.

ASSET ALLOCATION PLANS

Asset allocation is the method that determines how you divide your portfolio among different investments. It apportions your portfolio into different investment groups but does not show you which securities to hold in your portfolio. For example, what portion of your portfolio is going to be invested in mutual funds, stocks, bonds, and cash.

Asset allocation is a three-step process. First, determine your financial goals. Second, determine your investment profile based on the amount of risk you can handle and how much time you have to reach your goals. Third, decide how much of your total portfolio you'll place in each investment, based on your investment profile.

Although asset allocation plans vary among individuals, yours could take the shape of one of the following plans for an assumed $10,000 investment. The amount of your investment could, of course, be larger or smaller than $10,000.

PLAN # 1

Age Group	Type of Investment	Dollar Amount Invested	Percent of Investment
20s	Growth mutual fund	$3,000	30 percent
	Quality common stocks	$3,000	30 percent
	Money market fund	$4,000	40 percent

Asset allocation plan #1 is for the beginning investor—usually the single person with few responsibilities. The plan has the potential to provide a good long-term return with 30 percent of total assets invested in a growth mutual fund and 30 percent in quality common stocks, a somewhat risky investment. A large part of the $10,000 is held in a money market fund as a reserve for future investments. Asset allocation plan # 1 is for the person who has moderate to high risk tolerance.

PLAN # 2

Age Group	Type of Investment	Dollar Amount Invested	Percent of Investment
30s	Growth mutual fund	$2,500	25 percent
	Quality common stocks	$2,500	25 percent
	Zero-coupon bond fund	$4,000	40 percent
	Money market fund	$1,000	10 percent

Asset allocation plan #2 is for the person who has been employed for a few years and has pre-college children. It is a moderately conservative portfolio, but not to the point where it can't earn a good return. In this age group, capital growth is a major consideration, so 50 percent of the $10,000 portfolio is invested in a growth fund and common stocks. While 40 percent is allocated to a zero-coupon bond fund to help pay for college expenses. At this age level income may increase but so will expenses.

PLAN # 3

Age Group	Type of Investment	Dollar Amount Invested	Percent of Investment
40s	Growth mutual fund	$5,000	50 percent
	Quality common stocks	$2,500	25 percent
	Global fund	$1,000	10 percent
	Money market fund	$1,500	15 percent

Plan #3 is for the person who has well-defined investment goals—the person who has enough confidence to take an aggressive investment approach and yet maintain a relatively balanced portfolio. The percentage invested in a growth fund is more than in Plans # 1 and #2, enough to cover the down payment on a second home, supplement retirement income, or provide money for other goals. The person's children are out of college and on their own, so there is no longer a need for a zero-coupon bond fund. A global fund is added for foreign exposure and greater portfolio diversity. Plan #3 has the potential to fulfill medium to longer-term goals.

PLAN # 4

Age Group	Type of Investment	Dollar Amount Invested	Percent of Investment
50s	Growth mutual fund	$3,000	30 percent
	Index fund	$2,500	25 percent
	Quality common stocks	$2,500	25 percent
	Money market fund	$2,000	20 percent

Plan # 4 is for the person who wants to gratify goals such as traveling, a new home, or other ambitions. The global fund in plan # 3 is sold to reduce risk, and a more stable index fund is added to mirror a specific market index such as the S&P 500. At this age level, the person's earnings have probably reached their peak and there are fewer family responsibilities. This is the time to build assets that will supplement retirement income. Plan # 4 is a moderately conservative portfolio.

PLAN # 5

Age Group	Type of Investment	Dollar Amount Invested	Percent of Investment
60s	Growth mutual fund	$3,000	30 percent
	Series I bonds	$2,000	20 percent
	Growth & income fund	$2,500	25 percent
	Money market fund	$2,500	25 percent

Since retirement can present many financial uncertainties, plan #5 is for the retired person or someone about to retire. In plan # 5, the growth fund is maintained at the same level as Plan #4, but common stocks are sold and the proceeds are invested in a growth and income fund for greater safety. The money market fund is increased to 25 percent to pay for any unexpected emergencies. This is the time to reduce more speculative investments and to focus more on safety and income.

These asset allocation plans will not fit the requirements of all investors. Among the five plans, there can be considerable overlapping of investments. For example, though you might be in your 20s, there is no reason you cannot invest in bonds. And, if you are over 60, there is nothing wrong with investing in stocks. The asset allocation plans are merely intended to give you an idea of how asset allocation works. But remember, as your time horizon shortens, the safety of your money becomes an important factor. The last thing you want to do is hold risky investments when your children are ready for college. And when you near retirement, you might want to add safer investments such as bonds to your asset allocation plan.

There is one investment that is basic to most asset allocation plans— growth mutual funds. They have been discussed earlier, but deserve further review because they are relatively safe investments and generally provide a good return.

GROWTH MUTUAL FUNDS

Growth funds appeal to many investors in mutual funds. They can preserve your purchasing power against erosion from inflation and have the potential to provide a good return. They are especially appropriate when saving for college, housing, or retirement. After an emergency fund, you should consider a growth fund as your next investment.

Growth funds invest primarily in the common stock of companies that are expected to increase in market value at an accelerated rate, bonds, and cash equivalents for income and defensive purposes. In short, they are diversified.

Growth funds place more emphasis on capital gains and less importance on the payment of dividends. Since it's possible to earn a 15 percent to 20 percent average annual return investing in growth funds, probably no other investment can match their long-term appeal.

If you invest in a growth fund, don't let the day-to-day fluctuations of your fund disturb you. The secret for a good return on a growth fund is to invest regularly and reinvestment all dividends and capital gains paid by the fund to buy additional shares.

TIMING MUTUAL FUND INVESTMENTS

When is the best time to invest in mutual funds? The typical answer is to invest in funds when the prime interest rate (the preferential rate of interest on short-term loans by banks to their most creditworthy customers) is relatively low. When the prime rate is high, funds usually move down in price, and they rise when rates are low or going down. There is, of course, no proven method to determine when rates are at their peak or when they reach bottom.

At times you may be tempted to act on fluctuations in the price of a mutual fund. You could convince yourself to sell a fund when its price drops, then reinvest in the same fund when its price starts to rise. This is called timing the market, a skill that few investors possess. If your fund drops in price, it's better to stay invested and let your fund's manager time your investments.

One advantage of the DCAP formula is that it compensates you for any poorly timed investments in a mutual fund. Thus, don't let interest rates or a fund's price dictate when you will invest in a fund. Rather, make your first investment when you have the money and follow up with monthly investments using the DCAP formula.

CHAPTER 9
MANAGING YOUR PORTFOLIO

Once you decide which investments to include in your portfolio, you must decide whether you want to manage your portfolio or have someone else manage all or part of it. Being your own manager requires that you closely monitor the investments in your portfolio. It also requires that you have a basic understanding of capital gains, stock dividends, dividend reinvestment plans, and much more.

CAPITAL GAINS

Capital gains occur when the proceeds from the sale of a security exceed the cost of buying it. If you sell shares of a mutual fund or stock that you've owned for more than a year, you'll qualify for the long-term capital gains tax rate of 15 percent (5 percent if you are in the 10 percent or 15 percent tax bracket). However, if you sell shares you've owned for less than a year, your capital gains will be taxed at your regular tax rate.

When you sell shares of a stock, you must figure your gain or loss on the transaction. For example, suppose you bought one hundred shares of stock in XYZ Company at $20 a share and sold it two years later for $35. In this case, your capital gain is $1,500, less brokerage commission for buying and selling the stock.

Since you held the XYZ stock more than one year, you would pay 15 percent of your capital gains to the IRS if your tax bracket is 28 percent. If you had held the stock less than a year, your capital gains tax would be based on your regular tax bracket rate. If you are in the 28 percent tax bracket, then you pay 28 percent of your capital gains to the IRS.

There are four methods for computing capital gains when you sell shares in a mutual fund. Since they yield different results, before you redeem shares in a fund, you should project your tax using each of the methods, and then use the one that's best for you. These methods are discussed in greater detail later in this chapter.

To some people, the taxes on capital gains may seem excessive. Nevertheless, short-term capital gains on securities are taxed at the same rate as interest earned on savings accounts, money market mutual funds, and most other investments.

STOCK DIVIDENDS

The regular payment of a dividend increases the attractiveness of a stock. Although a company is not required to pay a dividend, they usually are paid when a company has good sales and earnings growth. A company's board of directors determines the amount of the dividend and the payment date. A company can pay its shareholders two kinds of dividends: cash and additional shares of stock in the company. A cash dividend is the stockholder's share of the company's profits. You can determine the yield (return) on a company's cash dividend by dividing the current price of the stock into the annual dividend payment. For instance, a stock priced at $20 that pays a yearly dividend of $1 yields 5 percent. Thus you can compare a stock's yield to the interest paid on bank savings accounts, bonds, and other investments to determine which has the better return.

When a company issues additional shares of stock to its shareholders, that is called a stock dividend or simply a stock split. For example, if you own 100 shares and a company splits its stock two for one, you have two hundred shares after the split. It's like trading a $10 bill for two $5 bills. Since all shareholders participate in the split, your percentage of ownership in the company is the same. And the value of your investment does not change, since the new shares would be half the price of the pre-split shares. Some companies issue stock dividends with or instead of cash dividends.

If you invest in common stocks, it's a good idea to consider closely a company's dividend record. Pay special attention to the dividend yield, frequency of increases (or decreases) in the dividend during the past several years, and any stock splits which can indicate a company's sales and earnings are increasing.

DIVIDEND REINVESTMENT PLANS

A high percentage of the companies that pay cash dividends have dividend reinvestment plans (DRIPs) that are attractive to many of their shareholders. DRIPs allow shareholders to reinvest all or part of their cash dividends to purchase additional shares of the company's stock, sometimes at a discount from the stock's market price. In addition, many companies allow their shareholders to make cash investments to buy additional shares of the company's stock. You can sell all or part of the shares you own in a DRIP back to the company at any time.

It's easy to invest in a DRIP. All you do is call for a company's prospectus and enrollment application. Complete the application and return it to the company. However, before you can enroll in a DRIP, usually you have to buy shares in the company through a stockbroker. What this means is that most companies with DRIPs do not handle an initial stock purchase directly.

WORKING WITH A BROKER

Regardless of the amount of money that you have to invest, you will be welcome when you contact a broker. If you are a beginning investor, know what you want before you talk to a broker. Knowing in advance, will save you time and you will not be persuaded to invest in something that doesn't interest you.

Full-service vs. Discount Brokerage Firms

There are two kinds of brokerage firms: full-service and discount. The full-service brokers as their name implies, offer a wide range of financial services to their clients. They make buy, sell, and hold recommendations on stocks, mutual funds, and other investments; provide research information on specific securities; and offer portfolio guidance to their clients.

The discount brokers, on the other hand, neither furnish their clients with research nor provide investment advice. They primarily execute buy and sell orders from their clients. Since discount brokers offer fewer services than full-service brokers, they charge much lower commissions. Discount brokers' commissions can be 50 percent to 70 percent less than those for full-service brokers.

It's not surprising that discount brokers cater to clients who prefer to manage their own portfolio. If you follow the suggestions in this book, you can easily manage your portfolio and a discount broker is all you'll need. However, if you need help when you invest, a full-service broker may be better for you.

Mutual Funds and Brokerage Firms

You can purchase mutual funds through discount brokers as well as full-service brokers. But full- service brokers sell almost exclusively load funds, while discount brokers, such as Charles Schwab and Company, handle both load and no-load funds.

You can buy shares in a mutual fund yourself, without the service of a full-service or discount broker. If you don't have the time or if you have problems with a fund's prospectus, then buy a no-load fund through a discount broker.

PORTFOLIO CHECKUP

As a motor tune-up can keep your car in good running condition, a review of your portfolio can keep it in shape. However, a review of your portfolio doesn't always mean it has to be overhauled.

If your portfolio has a mix of mutual funds, stocks, bonds, and money market funds, you should hold each investment to a separate performance standard. That's because different segments of the financial markets perform in very different ways over the long term.

It's a good practice to check your mutual fund monthly rather than daily. With a daily checkup, you could overreact to a short-term fluctuation in price. It's not a big job to check your fund's performance. After each investment, the fund will send you a financial statement that shows the number of shares you purchased, the purchase price, and total shares you own. The statement contains enough information so you can check the fund's performance.

Since stocks are generally a more risky investment than mutual funds, it's a good idea to check them daily. Any 10 percent decline in a stock below your purchase price is cause for concern.

Once you gather the information on your portfolio's performance, what do you do with it? First, compare the return on the investments in your portfolio with similar types of investments. For example, compare the performance of your mutual fund with the S&P 500 or another market index. Compare the return on your money market mutual fund with a money market deposit account at a bank. In short, compare your portfolio's return to similar investments and what you could have earned investing in them for the same period. If your return is less than that for comparable investments, maybe it's time to change the holdings in your portfolio.

If you've reviewed your portfolio, and you are satisfied with its performance, it's best to sit tight. Sometimes, staying the course and sticking to your investment objectives is an option that you will find usually pays off.

RE-BALANCING YOUR PORTFOLIO

Deciding on an asset allocation plan for your portfolio is not a one-time project. You should re-balance your portfolio for each stage of your life. The asset mix for someone who is single is different from that of a married person with children ready for college. For example, when your children are nearing college age, it's time to start selling your more risky investments and placing the proceeds in safer money market funds, bond funds, and other less risky investments. And as you approach retirement age, you may want less money in stocks and more in bond funds for safety and income.

You cannot re-balance your portfolio unless you have an asset allocation plan. The plans described in Chapter 8 suggest what portion of your assets could be held in various investment categories. Still, many asset allocation plans go further by dividing investments among narrower categories. For example, your stocks category could include subcategories such as growth, income, defensive, and speculative stocks. The mutual funds category could include growth, index, income, and global funds. And real estate could include two categories—your house and shares in a real estate investment trust.

As a rule, the more subcategories that you have in your asset allocation plan, the easier it will be to re-balance.

There are two ways to re-balance your portfolio. The first is to sell assets in one category and put the money in another category. For example, you could sell a growth fund and invest the proceeds in an index or money market fund. The second way is to invest new money to increase your holdings in categories that are under-weighted.

Here's how to determine if your portfolio should be re-balanced:

* List the total dollar value and the percentage of each investment category in your asset allocation plan. Be sure to include your retirement investments such as a 401 (k) and IRA.

* Compare the total dollar value of all categories and the percent invested in each category.

* If your percentages are not in line with your asset allocation plan, decide whether to sell part or all of an investment in a category or add new money to the category.

MANAGEMENT STRATEGIES

There are several strategies you can use to manage your portfolio. These range from earning the maximum growth on your mutual funds to maintaining good records on the investments in your portfolio.

Maximizing Grow with Mutual Funds

When you invest in a mutual fund, your goal should be to earn the maximum growth on your investment. The way to earn maximum growth is to: (1) invest regularly, (2) reinvest the dividends and capital gains paid by your fund, and (3) defer the payment of taxes on the dividends and capital gains that you receive from your fund.

Investing regularly is a difficult discipline, yet it is probably the best way to invest in a mutual fund. Once you start investing on a regular basis, it can become a habit very easily.

The reinvestment of dividends and capital gains is a kind of dollar-cost averaging because you buy more shares of a fund when the price is low. Most mutual funds have an automatic reinvestment plan (ARP) that allows you to reinvestment your dividends and capital gains. The use of an ARP is a good way to invest because it gives you the chance to acquire more shares in a fund and prevents you from spending the money if you receive it in cash.

The last way to get maximum growth from a fund is to defer taxes. You can do this if you make tax-deferred contributions to a mutual fund that's included in a retirement plan, such as 401(k) or an IRA.

When to Sell a Mutual Fund

The best strategy for investing in mutual funds is to buy those with a good track record and hold them for the long term. As important as long-term investing is to earning a good return, occasions do arise when it is wise to sell an underperforming fund.

If you invest in a mutual fund and it underperforms the market indexes, should you sell it? Before you decide whether or not to sell, here are some reasons why a fund could lag the market indexes.

* New management. Any time a fund changes managers, you should pay attention. A change of management does not mean a fund will perform poorly, but it does imply that a new manager may have an investment style that differs from the previous manager. You should be sure that the new manager isn't changing the fund into a different fund, one that differs from the reason you invested in it. For example, the new manager could be investing in more risky stocks that caused your fund to drop in price. In this case, it may be wise to sell your fund.

* The fund's investment style changes. In the prospectus, every fund states its objective. Thus, if the growth fund you invested in starts buying electric utility stocks, you've got a problem. In this case, the fund may be seeking dividends, rather than capital gains. It tells you that the fund is not sticking with its investment objective.

* The fund gets too big. Many times, small funds become large funds, and thus, may be difficult to manage. That does not mean that funds with large assets cannot provide a good return, but it does mean that many funds post their best returns when their assets are small. If your fund is large, and its return lags that of the market indexes, consider replacing it with a fund that has fewer assets.

Many mutual fund newsletters offer information on which funds to buy, but they seldom dispense advice on when to sell a fund. There is no proven method that determines when to sell a poor performing fund, but by observing a few warning signals, such as those mentioned above, usually you can decide when to exit an underperforming fund.

Selling Fund Shares

When you sell shares in a mutual fund, outside of a retirement account, the transaction must be reported to the IRS for the year the shares were sold. Under the tax laws, you have a choice of four methods for computing the cost basis on the fund shares that you sell.

* Average cost (single category). If you use the average cost single category method, your cost basis per share is the average cost

for all the shares of a fund that you sell. This is the most widely used method and easiest way to compute a fund's cost basis.

* First-in, first-out (FIFO). Using the FIFO method, let's you assume that you sold shares in the order that you purchased them. This is an easy method to use, but you must know the actual cost for the oldest shares sold.

* Average cost (double category). This method allows you to calculate your cost basis by the length of time you held your shares—instead of one average cost for all your shares, as used in the average cost single category. With the double category, you compute the average cost of shares you've held for a year or longer and shares held less than a year. The average cost double category method lets you fine-tune your cost basis.

* Specific shares method. With this method, you use the price of the specific shares you choose to sell as your cost basis. If you want to minimize taxes, select the highest cost shares. However, when you sell specific shares, you must notify your fund in advance that those are the shares to be sold.

Once you start to use a particular method for selling shares of a fund, you cannot switch to another method. However, you can use different cost basis methods for different funds.

Tax Saving Strategies

No one wants to pay more taxes than the law requires, yet many people do. There are legitimate tax saving strategies that could save you hundreds of dollars. Here are some strategies for reducing your taxes:

* If eligible, contribute to a tax-deferred retirement plan. Tax-deferred investments grow much faster than those which are taxable.

* Defer income to future years. To prevent a bunching of income when you are subject to higher taxes, you may be able to arrange a tax-deferred plan. Ways to defer income include deferred pay plans and installment sales when you sell property.

* Invest in tax-free bonds. A good way to receive tax-free income

is to invest in municipal bonds, which are not subject to taxes at the federal level and possibly not at the state level.

* Purchase Series EE and Series I bonds. The interest on EE and I bonds is exempt from state and local taxes. In addition, the interest on these bonds may be redeemed tax-free at the federal level, if you spend the proceeds for qualified higher education for yourself, your spouse, or your dependents.   * Shift income to a child who is in a lower tax bracket. This involves moving income from one family member (the parent) to another (the child) who is in a lower tax bracket.

* Exclude the gain on the sale of your home. If you sell your home at a gain, you may be able to exclude from gross income up to $250,000 of that gain ($500,000 if you are married filing a joint tax return).

* Take out a home equity loan. The advantage of a home equity loan is that the interest is tax deductible. Borrowing money on your home means you use as collateral that part of your home that you own, beyond any mortgage on the home.

The more money you pay in taxes the less you have to invest. The way you deal with taxes should depend on you investment goals and your financial situation. For example, if you expect your income to increase by an amount that would move you into a higher tax bracket, your tax planning would differ from someone who is retired, whose income may have stabilized.

Recordkeeping

It's important that you keep good records on the investments in your portfolio. They will come in handy for tax purposes. When you buy or sell securities, keep a record of all pertinent information such as the date of the transaction, number of shares bought or sold, the price, and any commission costs. As a shareholder in a mutual fund or stock, you own a part of the business, and good records are an essential part of doing business.

To sum up, managing your portfolio is not difficult, it can be educational, and it could prove very profitable. The first step in managing your portfolio is to determine your risk level, and then make sure you have the right investments to achieve your goals. After that, stay with your portfolio for the long term, making changes only when necessary.

CHAPTER 10
TOTAL FINANCIAL PLAN

A total financial plan covers all your family's needs. It includes requirements such as money set aside for emergencies, adequate insurance, housing, college expenses, retirement, estate planning, and your investments. As a rule, a total plan is usually not built all at once. Rather, you develop it through the years as your family needs dictate and money becomes available.

If you are just starting your financial plan, you probably have to stretch your paycheck to cover monthly expenses. In this case, you should set priorities on which of your family needs are the most important. Certainly, two of your top priorities should be to set money aside for emergencies and to provide adequate insurance for you and your family. After you cover these, the next priority will, of course, vary among individuals. For some, saving for the down payment on a house is next. Others may want to invest for their children's education. Once you have set your priorities, model your portfolio to attain them. Here are some family needs to consider when you set your priorities.

EMERGENCY FUND

There's no reason to have a financial plan until you have money set aside for unexpected emergencies. Where you invest your emergency money can make a difference. It's better to put your emergency dollars in a money market mutual fund than a passbook savings account. A money market fund is more attractive since it pays a higher return and is more difficult to draw on than a savings account.

LIFE INSURANCE

Before you invest, make sure that you have adequate life insurance. How do you determine if the insurance you have is enough? The answer, of course, is to look at your family's needs and the amount of life insurance you have now.

Think of life insurance as the way to maintain your family's living standard should anything happen to you. If something does happen, most financial experts agree that your family would need about 75 percent of its current net income to maintain the same living standard. When you figure your family's needs, include Social Security benefits and the cost of your children's education.

It's possible that you may have too much life insurance. Some people buy more insurance than they actually need. Few people without children need a large amount of life insurance. Remember, insurance is for protection, whether for the loss of a family head or business. So buy it as a protection against financial loss and not as an investment.

There are two basic kinds of life insurance: term and permanent. Let's look at them to see what they have to offer.

Term Insurance

Term insurance only provides death protection, and cash value is not built up. Over a short period, term insurance provides the most coverage at the least amount possible. However, the premiums (the cost) of term insurance increases substantially with your age until coverage is very costly when you are ready for retirement. Even so, some term policies are convertible, which means you can switch to a permanent policy later on.

Permanent Insurance

Permanent insurance is available in four types—whole, adjustable, universal, and variable. They all provide similar coverage, including a death benefit and tax-deferred cash accumulation. The main difference among the different types is the ability to borrow or withdraw money from the policy, and how much flexibility you have in managing the features of the policy.

The type of life insurance that most people need will, of course, vary. The single person may not need any insurance. The married person with no children may need only a small term policy. A person with a family may need term insurance that is convertible to a permanent policy later on.

Buying Insurance

When you buy life insurance, be careful. Within the last few years, some insurance companies have had financial problems. This raises the question, what if I outlive the insurance company? Fortunately, you can take some precautions to improve your chances of avoiding an insurance company that's shaky.

First, know which insurance company is behind the policy you are considering. Then check the company's credibility in either Best's Insurance Reports, Standard and Poor's, or Duff and Phelps. These publications, available at most libraries, rate insurance companies according to their financial strength. Always buy your insurance from a financially strong company.

Second, consider whether to diversify by buying policies from two or three different companies instead of a large policy from one company, thus reducing risk.

Third, if you have group coverage at work, it's probably better to get your insurance there—assuming that your employer has chosen a financially strong insurance company.

Finally, compare insurance policies on the Web. Here are some Web sites that provide information about insurance:

Insure.com www.insure.com

InsWeb www.insweb.com

Intelliquote www.intelliquote.com

InsureMarket www.insuremarket.com

Quotesmith www.quotesmith.com

ReliaQuote www.insureclick.com

SAVINGS AND INVESTING

Which is the best way to reach your goals, to put your money in a savings account or to invest it in mutual funds and stocks? Or does it make any difference? You bet it makes a difference.

Over the course of several years, it can make a big difference because saving rather than investing usually provides a lower return on your money. Let's look at the numbers. The inflation rate has averaged around 5 percent over the last thirty years. Suppose you put $1,000 into a savings account in 1975 with an average return of 3 percent. What would have happened to your $1,000 over those thirty years? It would have increased to $2,456 before taxes. Today, you need about $4,800 to match the buying power of your $1,000.

If you had invested $1,000 in a mutual fund that returned 15 percent annually, your money would have grown to $87,541 over the thirty years. Even better, a one-time investment of $10,000 in a mutual fund that returned 15 percent would have increased to about $875,000 thirty years later.

You should realize that savings and investing work together. You save and then you invest your savings. And the best way to keep ahead of inflation is to invest most of your savings to earn dividends and capital gains.

Savings

It can be tough to save money regularly. But even saving a few extra dollars monthly can mean thousands later on. For example, skipping your espresso coffee each day can save you more than $8 a week, or about $35 a month. That doesn't sound like much but investing $35 a month in your IRA at a 9 percent annual return for 30 years will give you an extra $64,500.

How much money should you regularly save? Should you set aside savings weekly, monthly, or on paydays? Since most people have different ideas about saving money, it depends on factors like your age, health, number and ages of your children, your pay schedule, where you plan to save, and your goals.

Where to Save

There are basically four places to set aside savings—banks, savings and loan associations, credit unions, and money market mutual funds. Let's see what each has to offer.

(1) Banks. The passbook savings account that banks offer are safe, liquid, and convenient. However, banks generally pay a lower rate of return than what you can receive elsewhere. Bank saving accounts are insured to $100,000 by the Federal Deposit Insurance Corporation (FDIC).

(2) Savings and loan associations. These are financial institutions established mainly to offer home loans and savings accounts. Deposits are easy to make and withdrawals are readily accessible. Deposits are insured to $100,000 by the Federal Savings and Loan Association Insurance (FSLIC).

(3) Credit unions. Credit unions can be either federal or state chartered. They are cooperatives formed by members of a specific group such as a company, church, or labor union. Credit union savings accounts are usually restricted to employees of the organization sponsoring the credit union. Their deposits are insured to $100,000 by the National Credit Union Association (NCUA).

(4) Money market mutual funds(MMMFs). MMMFs invest in CDs, commercial paper (short-term IOUs) issued by large corporations, treasury securities, and bankers' acceptances that finance international commercial transactions.

Although MMMFs are not insured, they are one of the best places to build savings. Your deposits in a MMMF are liquid, which means you can easily convert your shares into cash with the use of a check-writing privilege. You can use them to pay bills (although the minimum amount for writing checks is usually $500), as an emergency fund, and as a source for tax-free income if you invest in a tax-free MMMF. Except for tax-free funds, the interest earned on a MMMF is about one-half to 1 percent higher than what bank passbook savings accounts offer.

How to Save

If it's hard for you to save money, set up a savings schedule. The advantage of a schedule is that it gets you in the habit of setting aside part of your income that you can eventually use for investing.

A reasonable and meaningful amount to save each month is 10 percent of your gross income. But you don't have to set aside 10 percent right after you start saving. If you prefer, you can start slowly setting aside two percent the first three months then increase your savings every three months by two percent. At the end of fifteen months, you'll reach your 10 percent savings goal. Here's how it works.

Savings Schedule

Monthly Percent to Save	Number of Months to Save
2 percent	3 months
4 percent	3 months
6 percent	3 months
8 percent	3 months
10 percent	3 months
Goal: 10 percent	Total months: 15

If you are not saving at least 10 percent of your gross income, the way to get started is to reduce your living expenses. That means you'll have to cut your expenses two percent every three months until you are saving 10 percent.

Investing

The old-fashioned way of leaving all your money in a savings account, no longer applies. Today, if you want to receive a good return, you must invest as well as save money.

Historically, the better investments have been (1) a business, (2) your home and other real estate, (3) stocks, and (4) mutual funds. If you already own real estate, and don't have a business, that only leaves stocks and mutual funds as investment alternatives. But mutual funds have an advantage over stocks because of the diversification they offer. With funds, the success of your investment isn't dependent upon the outcome of one company's stock. In fact, stock mutual funds have been referred to as probably the best investment available.

If you invest your savings in a mutual fund, it's possible to earn a good profit on your money. Through the years, many funds have provided an above-average return when you compare them to the traditional places, such as savings account, where many people invest their money.

HOUSING

Whether you own or rent, housing is an important part of any investment program. Keep in mind that a house is first a place to live and then an investment. What's more, a house is not a liquid asset. At times, it can be almost impossible to sell a house at the asking price.

In the past, the prices of many houses have greatly increased. However, there is no assurance that they will continue to go up in price. In fact, in a few areas, houses are below their purchase price. Whether or not you are a home owner, here are some advantages and disadvantages to owning a home.

* A house can provide security and stability. When you rent there is always the possibility that you may have to move.

* A house usually has more living space than an apartment and fewer restrictions.

* There are financial benefits when you own a house, since property taxes and mortgage interest are tax deductible. Also,

when you pay the mortgage each month, you pay both interest and principal. The principal repayments, plus any increase in house value, builds up your equity in the property—the difference in what you owe and the value of the house.

* If you sell your house at a gain, you may be able to exclude from gross income up to $250,000 of that gain if single or $500,000 if married filing a joint tax return.

* Owning a house brings a feeling of satisfaction to many people.

* There is no guarantee that you can sell your house for more than the purchase price.

* When you rent, your money is not tied up in the down payment on a house.

* If you are a home owner, there will be maintenance costs such as roof repairs, plumbing, painting, and other upkeep.

The decision whether or not to rent or buy a house is primarily a matter of personal preference and available resources. If you don't expect to live in a house more than three to five years, renting is usually more economical than buying.

INVESTING FOR COLLEGE

It's no secret that college is expensive, and the price is likely to continue to rise. The cost of a year at a public college rose 8 percent in 2004, far in excess of the inflation rate. By the time your children are ready for college, they could be facing costs of $20,000 a year.

You can't rely too much on financial aid such as grants, scholarships, and student loans to pay for college expenses. These programs may have eligibility requirements that not all students and their families can meet. However, there are other ways to help finance your children's education. Here are some of them.

Home Equity Credit Line

A home equity credit line is a flexible arrangement and may be useful to finance your children's education. In this type of arrangement, the lender puts you through a full mortgage checkup. If you qualify, you receive a line of credit that may extend for four years or perhaps indefinitely.

But, there are warnings. Make sure you understand all the rules and don't forget the lender has a lean on your house.

Education Unitrust
An education unitrust provides a way for parents or grandparents to transfer an appreciated asset into a special education trust. The donor will receive a charitable tax deduction and may even bypass capital gains taxes. A unitrust should be designed so the student receives income from the unitrust at regular intervals, covering the length of the student's college years.

Income Shifting
The Tax Reform Act of 1998 allows you to shift investment income from yourself to your children, which can help with college expenses. The act provides that a child under the age of 14 can be taxed at the child's rate not the parent's rate, on the total of investment income (interest and dividends) below $1,600. The $1,600 figure is adjusted upward each year to account for inflation.

Uniform Transfer to Minors Act
The Uniform Transfer to Minors Act (UTMA) is another way to help pay for college. Under the UTMA, a custodial account is set up with a bank, mutual fund, or brokerage firm to achieve income splitting. Income from a custodian account is generally taxed at the child's rate, rather than the parent's rate. These easy-to-set up accounts allow parental control of the money until the child reaches a certain age usually 18 or 21, depending on state law.

Series EE and Series I Bonds
You may be able to exclude all or a portion of the interest received (upon redemption) of your Series EE and I bonds, if you use the interest to pay for qualified education expenses. You aren't required to indicate

that you intend to use the bonds for educational purposes when you purchase them, although you should ensure that you comply with the program's requirements.

Zero-coupon Bonds

You can use specifically laddered treasury zero-coupon bonds to help fund your children's education. Zero-coupons can be bought in the child's name so income will be taxable to the child, presumably at a lower tax rate than yours. Still, in today's dollars, it would require a large investment to ensure there's enough money to cover college expenses when the bonds mature.

Coverdell Education Savings Account

Coverdell Education Savings Accounts (ESAs) allow you to make contributions of up to $2,000 for each child per year to save for college. The earnings on ESAs grow tax-free and withdrawals are also tax-free if the proceeds are used for qualified higher education costs for the covered child. Contributions to the ESA must end when the child reaches age 18.

College Annuity Option

A college annuity option could be set up as a deferred gift annuity, payable when your children reach college age. The annuity would be payable in four or five installments each year your children are in college. You would still have to pay capital gains tax on the assets, but the charitable gift deduction would probably offset that tax.

State Plans

All states have tax-deferred education plans, referred to as "529 plans." These plans, designated as either prepaid or as savings plans, are run by states to provide savings for college. Prepaid plans let you lock in college tuition rates by paying now for a future education. While savings plans let you set up an account from which college expenses can be paid. Both plans have professional money managers and state and federal taxes are deferred until the money is withdrawn, when it is taxed at the student's rate. If the money isn't spent for education, you lose the tax benefits and incur a penalty.   If you have access to the Web, you can get information about investing for college at these Web sites:

College Board On-line www.collegeboard.com

CollegeQuest www.collegequest.com

Fastweb.com www.fastweb.com

FinAid www.finaid.com

Kaplan www.kaplan.com

The Princeton Review www.review.com

Mutual Funds

For the relatively small investor, mutual funds can help with college costs. In fact, the use of mutual funds has become the investment of choice to pay for a child's education. If you decide on funds, look for those with good long-term returns of 15 percent or better, no front-end load, 12b-1 fee, or back-end load, plus low minimum and subsequent investment requirements. If you start investing in funds when your children are young, you should be able to cover most if not all of your children's college expenses.

When your children are nearing college age, you probably shouldn't commit money to mutual funds for their education. That is the time to switch from mutual funds to money market funds to reduce your risk exposure.

RETIREMENT

It's never too early to start investing for retirement. Since a comfortable retirement isn't something that just happens, you should begin investing for it several years before you leave your job.

How much will you need to live comfortably in retirement? Many people say it will require about 75 percent of the income you earn before retirement to maintain an equivalent standard of living. When you retire, your housing, clothing, transportation, and taxes will probably be less, but medical expenses may be higher.

Where will your retirement money come from? For most people, it will originate from a company retirement plan, Social Security, and personal investments. If you have a company retirement plan, it will cover about 50 percent to 60 percent of your retirement expenses. If you are eligible for Social Security, it will cover even less. That means, for a comfortable retirement, you will have to start saving for it before you retire. Here is a description of the more popular retirement plans.

Social Security

Social Security provides monthly payments for life to qualifying wage earners. It pays some on Medicare costs, reduces benefits for people retiring early, and reduces payments to those who earn more than a specific amount in retirement. You must contribute to Social Security for at least forty quarters or the equivalent of ten years to be eligible for benefits. Since Social Security probably won't cover all your expenses in retirement, you will need other sources of income.

You should be aware that the age for receiving full Social Security benefits, traditionally 65, is now increasing by a few months each year. For example, if your 65 birthday is in 2005, full benefits will not be available until you are 65 and 6 months. You'll still be able to start collecting reduced benefits at age 62, but the amount will gradually be reduced.

401 (k) Plan

The 401(k) plan is the most popular and fastest growing of all retirement plans. The plan, set up by your employer, is tax-deferred until you make withdrawals. Your contributions to a 401 (k) are not included in your gross income, but they are subject to Social Security and Medicare taxes.

There are several names for 401 (k) plans. They may be called a "retirement income fund," "retirement plan," or simply "savings plan." Whatever the name, these plans are established under Section 401 (k) of the Internal Revenue Service Code.

You can contribute to a 401 (k) through payroll deduction. However, there is a limit to the salary reduction contributions you can make to your 401 (k). For 2005, the limit is $14,000 and an additional $4,000 for people 50 and older. Your employer may also contribute to your 401 (k), either with a matching contribution or profit-sharing plan.

Many 401 (k) plans offer participants a choice of investments and the chance to change them. You may have investment choices that include: stocks, bonds, and mutual funds; guaranteed investment contracts; and your company's stock. Since a 401 (k) is a good way to save for retirement, take advantage of it should you have the opportunity.

Keogh Plan

If you are self-employed, you may be eligible to open a Keogh plan for your retirement. You can contribute to a Keogh if you're in business for yourself, whether it's part-time or full-time. There are two types of Keogh plans: defined-benefit and defined-contribution. The main difference between the two is that the defined-contribution plan sets limits on what goes in your account, while the defined-benefit plan has no limitation. Which of these plans is better for you depends on your age and other factors. If you set up a Keogh, you must designate a trustee, such as a mutual fund, brokerage firm, or bank to administer the plan.

Like the 401 (k) plan, a Keogh plan offers tax-deferred savings until you withdraw them and the opportunity to deduct contributions from your taxable income. Your contributions to a Keogh are limited to a dollar amount or percentage of your annual income.

Since a Keogh is an ideal way for you to save for retirement and reduce your taxable income, make a full contribution to one if you qualify.

Simplified Employee Pension–Individual Retirement Account

A Simplified Employee Pension-Individual Retirement Account (SEP-IRA) is both a retirement plan and type of IRA. The plan combines the main features of an IRA and a Keogh plan. If you are self-employed, you can open a SEP-IRA or your employer can open one if you qualify. If your employer opens a SEP-IRA for you, it could be linked to the company's retirement and profit-sharing plan.   Your contributions to a SEP-IRA are vested and not taxable income until withdrawn. If you are eligible, it makes sense for you to contribute to a SEP-IRA. Your contributions will lower your taxable income and maximize your retirement savings.

Savings Incentive Match Plan

The Savings Incentive Match Plan (SIMPLE) is a retirement plan for small employers. This plan allows your employer to establish a SIMPLE for qualified employees as part of a 401 (k).

Under a SIMPLE, your employer is required to match your contribution to the plan on a dollar-for-dollar basis up to three percent. Your contributions to the plan are based on a percent of your compensation and cannot exceed $14,000 for year 2005, plus an additional $4,000 if you are 50 or older. Also, your contributions are excluded from your income and your plan's earnings are tax deferred. Distributions from a SIMPLE are taxed under the rules for IRA distributions.

Profit-sharing Plan

Profit-sharing plans *allow* your company to contribute a portion of its year-end profits into a fund for your retirement. The maximum contribution to a profit-sharing account cannot exceed 25 percent of your annual compensation, with a limit of $40,000. As a company employee, you're not required to contribute to a profit-sharing plan.

A profit-sharing plan usually offers you the choice to invest in you company's stock, mutual funds, and fixed-income securities. In addition to profit-sharing, your employer may offer you another type of retirement plan such as a 401 (k).

Employee Stock Ownership Plan

An employee stock ownership plan (ESOP) is similar to a profit-sharing plan. However, an ESOP *allows* your company to contribute shares of its stock to a trust account held in your name. Thus, you can accumulate company stock at little or no cost and become a company owner.

In addition to your company's contribution, many ESOPs will allow you to buy additional shares of company stock. The maximum yearly contribution you and your employer can make to an ESOP is 25 percent of your salary up to $30,000. You are fully vested with the company after five or seven years, and you have the choice whether to rollover your ESOP to an IRA if you leave the company.

An ESOP can be a good retirement plan, if your company's stock increases in price, but what if it drops in price? In that case, an ESOP could wreck your plans for retirement. So it's wise to have other investments, such as an IRA, in case the price of your company's stock drops.

403(b) Plan

403(b) retirement plans are offered by public schools and tax-exempt organizations. Participants include teachers, nurses, doctors, researchers, and ministers. With a 403(b) plan, you set aside money for retirement on a pre-tax basis through a salary reduction agreement with your employer. You can choose from the investments offered by your employer where your money will be invested. Your money grows tax-free until withdrawals at retirement.

If your employer also contributes to your 403(b), the contributions are tax-free only if they do not exceed the annual limit on contributions to a defined contribution plan, which for 2004 was the lesser of 100 percent of compensation or $41,000.

Individual Retirement Account

Individual Retirement Accounts (IRAs) are available to all wage earners whether or not they have another retirement plan. You have the choice of three types of IRAs: traditional; Roth; or a combination of the two IRAs.

You can contribute to a traditional IRA if you receive taxable income and you are under age 701/2. Your contributions to a traditional IRA can be deductible or nondeductible from your income, and the earnings accrue tax-deferred until distribution, when they are taxed as ordinary income.

The minimum age at which you can receive payments from a traditional IRA without paying taxes and a penalty is 59 1/2, unless there are special circumstances such as disability. You must start withdrawing your money from a traditional IRA by April 1 following the year you are 70 1/2 and stick to a minimum withdrawal schedule.

With a Roth IRA, your contributions are not tax-deductible but earnings accumulate tax-free. Additionally, unlike a traditional IRA, you can make contributions to a Roth IRA after age 70 1/2 and there is no minimum withdrawal schedule.

Since your contributions to a Roth IRA are from your after-tax income, you can withdraw them at any time without paying taxes or a penalty. Moreover, there are no taxes or penalty on the earnings you withdraw if your account has been established over five years and you are over age 59 1/2.

You can set up a traditional IRA one year and choose a Roth IRA the next year. You also may split your contributions between the two types of IRAs.

Choosing an IRA

Deciding whether to choose a traditional IRA, Roth IRA, or a combination of the two IRAs, can be a tough decision. You should consider a Roth IRA if you have a medium to long-term investment horizon of more than five years until you retire. Also, a Roth IRA may be best if you don't qualify for a deductible, traditional IRA.

On the other hand, a deductible, traditional IRA may be your best choice if you want a long-term retirement plan designed to provide maximum tax-deferred growth.

Choosing between a traditional and Roth IRA also depends on your tax rate at retirement. A Roth IRA will probably generate more after-tax income than a traditional IRA if you are in a high tax bracket in retirement.

As it turns out, IRAs are good investments because your assets grow tax-deferred until you withdraw them. For example, if you invest $200 a month in an IRA, and receive an 8 percent return, you will accumulate about $117,000 after twenty years.

ESTATE PLANNING

Once you set up your financial plan, consider an estate plan to transfer your assets to your beneficiaries should anything happen to you. An estate plan ensures that your assets will be distributed according to your wishes.

You'll probably find that an estate plan requires adjustments from time to time to reflect changes in your family situation. Also, you'll need the help of an adviser such as an attorney or banker to make it legal.

Making a Will

Regardless of the amount of your assets, you should have a will. If you die intestate (without a will) what will happen to your estate? A court in your state will appoint someone to distribute your assets. If you are married, it would probably be your surviving spouse. If you were the surviving spouse, one of your children would probably distribute your assets. If there is no relative to distribute your estate, the court would appoint a public administrator. In that case, your estate is divided among your relatives.

When you make a will, you must name an executor (personal representative) for your estate. The executor is responsible for distributing your assets as you directed and administering other aspects of your will. The executor of an estate receives a fee, set by state law, that usually ranges between 1 and 3 percent of the estate's value.

An estate for which there are children or elderly dependents could require an executor for several years. During this period, the executor might be unable to continue to administer your estate. In that case, you should name a successor executor at the time you draw up your will. If a successor isn't named, the court would appoint one who might not handle your estate as you desired.

Once you make a will, don't put it away and forget about it. Review it regularly to make sure a revision of the tax laws, a change in your family situation or that of your heirs, won't affect the terms of your will.

The thing to do is to make a will and review it often. If you die without one, your estate will be distributed according to the laws of the state where you lived, not according to your wishes.

Probate

Probate is a legal process that a will must pass through before assets are distributed to beneficiaries. The executor named in the will is responsible for proving to the court that the will is valid and for carrying out the terms of the will.

Before a will is probated, the court determines whether the will is legally written, assures that debts are paid, and oversees the proceedings of the executor until the probate process is completed. It usually takes six to eight months for a will to be probated.

You can avoid probate by keeping your assets beyond the jurisdiction of the court. This is done by transferring ownership of your assets during your lifetime. For example, you can use joint tenancy, trusts, gifts, and retirement plans to transfer your assets.

JOINT TENANCY

Joint tenancy with right of survivorship is probably the best way to avoid probate. Any asset—a house, an automobile, or bank account, with more than one name on the ownership document, is joint tenancy. Thus, the survivor receives title of ownership at the death of the co-owner. It's important that the ownership document states "joint tenancy with right of survivorship." Otherwise, the document may have to be probated.

TRUSTS

A trust is a legal document that serves a variety of purposes for estate planning and avoiding probate. It will allow you to transfer the benefits of your assets while leaving the legal ownership of the assets in the trust. You could, for example, use a trust to set aside money for minor children, make gifts to charity, protect a business, or assure lifelong income for a spouse. If you decide on a trust, know what you want it to accomplish and then talk to a lawyer about establishing one.

Here are some points to consider if you set up a trust:

(1) With a trust, you'll need to name a trustee. A trustee is responsible for administering the trust according to your instructions. There have been situations when an individual was the trustee and assets of the trust were misused or stolen. So it's probably better to name a bank as the trustee. If a bank employee violates the trust, presumably the bank will make restitution.

(2) If you name a bank as the trustee, give your beneficiaries the power to substitute another bank. The power to change banks is important since it could protect your estate from an inefficient bank.

(3) If you have minor children and you set up a living trust, you still need a simple will. This is because your minor children will need a guardian.

(4) A trust should have a pour-over will to cover any assets you might forget to place in the trust. Any assets not included in the trust must go through probate.

There are several kinds of trusts all designed to ensure that your assets are distributed according to your wishes. Here are some of the more common types:

Credit Shelter Trust

A Credit Shelter Trust (also called a bypass trust) is a receptacle for property that will pass tax-free to beneficiaries under the federal estate tax exemption of $1,500,000 per donor. It is one of the most familiar types of trusts and helps both husband and wife since it allows the surviving spouse, as the primary beneficiary, to benefit from the trust without the property being included in the estate.

Qualified Terminable Interest Property Trust

With a Qualified Terminable Interest Property Trust (QTIP), the trust agreement, not the spouse, controls who gets the assets at death. What happens to the deceased's estate at death depends on what the trust specifies. For example, the trust might specify that the spouse will receive income from the trust, but at the spouse's death the principal in the trust would pass to the beneficiaries named.

Grantor Retained Annuity Trust

Another way to distribute your assets is with a Grantor Retained Annuity Trust (GRAT), an irrevocable trust, that let's you transfer property to the trust for a fixed number of years. It is possible, for example, to establish a GRAT on your home for your beneficiaries. In this case, you place your home in a trust and continue to live in the home. The beneficiaries of the trust will receive the home when the trust expires. In case the beneficiaries die before the trust expires, the home is placed back into your estate.

Charitable Remainder Trust

With a charitable remainder trust, you can leave appreciated assets to a charitable organization and receive a partial tax deduction. You could, for example, leave stocks valued at $50,000 to a charity. When you set up the trust, you can stipulate that a beneficiary be paid a yearly amount from the trust's income and have a charity control the property until the trust terminates. In the meantime, you avoid paying a capital gains tax on any increase in the value of the stocks, you get a charitable tax deduction, and the beneficiary receives income from the trust until it terminates. When the trust terminates, the charity receives the property.

GIFTS

You can reduce your tax liability by giving up to $11,000 to an unlimited number of persons. You can give $11,000 each year and the amount can be doubled to $22,000 if you are married and your spouse consents to "split" the gifts.

As you might expect, there can be problems with gifts. One problem is when a house is given to someone and the donor lives in it rent-free. In this case, the IRS will consider the house part of the estate. Another area the IRS will challenge is the gift of stocks and bonds when the donor continues to receive dividends and interest from the securities.

With gifts, you need to plan carefully to assure that they are made in compliance with IRS rules. Also, it's not wise to hand out gifts if you may need the property later on.

RETIREMENT BENEFITS

You can include the benefits of your retirement plan in your estate. These benefits are outside the court's jurisdiction and pass directly to your beneficiaries.

Since much of your estate's assets may come from your retirement plan, a unified credit shelter trust could protect it from federal estate taxes. To set up a unified credit shelter trust, you'll probably need to contact someone who is an expert in both estate and retirement planning.

A Roth IRA is more than a savings vehicle for retirement. Unlike a traditional IRA, the unspent funds in a Roth IRA belong to your beneficiaries and can continue to grow tax-free. Another feature is that your beneficiaries pay no income taxes on money received from a Roth IRA. Whereas, beneficiaries would pay taxes on money received from a traditional IRA.

Estate planning can be difficult, so you'll probably need the services of professionals. A lawyer can handle the legal aspects of your estate and help you determine which documents, such as wills, trusts, and gifts, would be the best way to distribute your assets. A tax accountant can help you minimize federal estate and gift taxes. And an insurance agent could review your insurance needs to provide protection for your family.

LIFETIME INVESTING

Many people cultivate a lifelong habit of investing. These are the people who regularly set aside money to achieve their goals. They take charge of their finances and know the difference between the return on a mutual fund and that on a bond.

Unfortunately, other people consider investing as socking away a few hundred dollars in a CD and rolling it over into a new CD when the old one matures. They often spend so much time on not losing money that they seldom think about how to make it. Usually, these are the people who lack an investment plan and don't understand risk..

Develop an Investment Plan

Before you invest, set realistic goals, then develop an investment plan. Once you have a plan, determine how much money you can invest each month to achieve your goals. Investing is similar to taking a trip. First you decide where you want to go and then you plan how you are going to get there.

One purpose of this book is to help you develop and manage your personal investment plan. To get you started, five asset allocation plans were suggested. During your lifetime, your plan could take many detours from what you originally designed. For example, when you have children ready for college, your plan will be different from the one you developed when you were first married.

Determine your Risk Level

Most investments are risky. Usually, the greater the potential return, the greater the risk. Thus, the main barrier when you invest is the risk factor—the chance that you will lose money. You are the best judge of your tolerance for risk. Once you know your tolerance, use it as a guide when you invest. Regardless of the potential return on an investment, if it makes you uncomfortable, you should consider other investments.

Investment Selections

The list of investment choices in Chapter 2 does not cover every way you can invest. It is confined to investments that are less risky, with special emphasis on mutual funds since they offer several advantages over many other types of investments.

Mutual funds can meet the needs of just about any type of investor. Many funds have low to moderate risk and may provide you with a good return on your money. Also, it's easy to open an account with a fund and you can add small amounts to your fund on a regular basis. If the ideal investment portfolio exits, it might contain the following investments:

* No-load mutual funds.

* Quality common stocks.

* U.S. government bond funds and municipal bond funds.

* Money market mutual funds.

GLOSSARY OF INVESTMENT TERMS

Account

A bookkeeping record of a client's transactions with an investment firm. It includes a client's credit and debit balances of cash and securities.

Annuity

Investment offered by life insurance companies. The annuitant receives regular income for life, or a fixed period, in exchange for a one-time payment or installment payments.

Appreciation

An increase in an investment's value.

Asset

Any item of value owned by an individual or corporation.

Asset allocation

Dividing a portfolio among several investments that are affected by different degrees of risk and economic conditions.

Automatic reinvestment plan (ARP)

An option available to mutual fund shareholders by which their dividends and capital gains are invested to buy additional shares in a fund.

Automatic withdrawal

An option available to mutual fund shareholders that allows them to receive a fixed dollar amount of their assets periodically.

Back-end load

A fee charged by some mutual funds when a shareholder redeems shares.

Bear market

A period when security prices in a particular market (such as the stock market) are generally falling for an extended period of time; the opposite of a bull market.

Beneficiary

The person who receives an inheritance from a trust, retirement plan, or insurance policy.

Bond

A debt security in the form of a loan from the bondholder to a corporation or municipality. The bondholder receives interest payments on the loan.

Bond fund

A collection of bonds issued by several companies with varying maturity dates and managed by an investment company.

Broker (stockbroker)

A person or firm that acts as an intermediary between buyers and sellers of securities.

Bull market

A period when security prices in a particular market (such as the stock market) are generally going up for an extended period of time; the opposite of a bear market.

Capital gain or loss

The difference between the price at which you buy an investment and the price at which you sell it.

Capital gains distribution

Profits distributed to shareholders resulting from the sale of securities held in a mutual fund's portfolio.

Certificate of deposit (CD)

A certificate issued for money deposited at a bank or savings and loan for a specific period of time at a specific rate of interest.

Closed-end fund

A managed investment fund with a fixed number of shares traded in the securities markets through brokers.

Collateral

An asset used to secure a loan. If the loan is not repaid, the asset may be seized.

Commission

A fee charged by a broker for buying and selling securities for an individual or investment firm.

Commodities

Bulk goods such as metals, oil, grain, and livestock traded on a commodities exchange.

Common stock

Securities that represent ownership in a company, issued in units of shares.

Conversion privilege (exchange privilege)

The right of a mutual fund shareholder to switch from one fund to another.

Corporate bond fund

A mutual fund that invests primarily in the bonds of corporations.

Custodial account

An account that is set up for a child by an adult, and used for tax purposes.

Custodian (trustee)

An organization that holds investments for safekeeping. All IRAs and Keogh plans require a custodian.

Defined-benefit plan

A pension plan paid for by the employer and guaranteed by the Pension Benefit Guaranty Corporation. A defined-benefit plan pays a fixed amount to qualified employees at retirement.

Defined-contribution plan

An employer-sponsored plan that pays retirement benefits to qualified employees. The benefit amount is based on the performance of investments in the plan.

Discount broker

A brokerage firm that handles buy and sell orders from customers and charges a lower commission   than a full-service broker. See full-service broker.

Distributions

Dividends, interest, and capital gains paid to mutual fund shareholders.

Diversification

A method of investing that involves buying several securities to reduce risk.

Dividend

A payment by a company in the form of cash, stock, or assets to its shareholders.

Dividend reinvestment plan

A program under which a company automatically reinvests a shareholder's cash dividends in additional shares of common stock. Also called a DRIP.

Dollar-cost averaging

A method of investing equal amounts at regular intervals.

Dollar-Cost Averaging Plus (DCAP)

A formula for investing varying amounts in an open-end mutual fund.

Dow-Jones averages

A measure of stock market price movements based on thirty industrials, twenty transportation, and fifteen utility stocks.

Earnings per share

A company's profits after taxes, bond interest, and preferred stock payments have been subtracted, divided by the number of shares of common stock outstanding.

Equities
Stocks, real estate, and other assets that an investor owns, but not bonds, since an investor lends money for their purchase.

Estate
1. All real and personal property in which a person has an interest.
2. The assets and liabilities left by a person at death.

Expense ratio
A mutual fund's cost of doing business, expressed as a percent of its assets.

Family of funds
A group of mutual funds, each having a different investment objective, but managed by the same investment company. A family usually consists of stock, bond, and money market funds.

Fixed-income fund
A mutual fund that invests primarily in bonds and preferred stock.

401 (K)
A tax-deferred employee retirement plan provided by an employer.

Front-end load
A sales charge that investors pay when buying shares of some mutual funds. See no-load mutual fund.

Full-service broker
A broker who handles buy and sell orders, research, and other services for clients. See discount broker.

Global-equity fund

A mutual fund that invests in securities traded worldwide, including the U.S.

GNMA fund

A mutual fund that invests in debt securities of the Government National Mortgage Association.

Government securities

Generic name for U.S. government securities which include treasury bills, notes, and bonds; Series EE, HH, and I bonds; certificates of indebtedness for interbank and interagency transfers of funds; and agency securities such as Federal National Mortgage Association (FNMA), and Government National Mortgage Association (GNMA).

Growth fund

A mutual fund that invests mainly in the common stock of companies whose sales and earnings are growing. These funds tend to invest in stocks that are expected to increase in value asopposed to those that pay a relatively high dividend.

Growth and income fund

A mutual fund that invests in the common stock of established companies that have increasing share value and a record of paying relatively high dividends.

Growth stock

The common stock of a company whose sales and earnings are increasing in value at a relatively rapid rate.

Index

A measurement of stock market price movement. Examples are Dow-Jones Industrial Average, Standard and Poor's 500, and NASDAQ Composite Index.

Index fund

A mutual fund with a portfolio of securities that includes many of the same stocks as those in an index such as the Dow-Jones Industrial Average, Standard and Poor's 500, and NASDAQ.

Individual retirement account (IRA)

A tax-deferred retirement plan for employed persons.

Inflation

An increase in the selling cost of goods and services resulting in a decrease in the value of what a dollar will buy of these goods and services.

Inflation risk

The chance that a portion of an investment's return may be limited by inflation.

Interest rate

The rate of payment, expressed as a percentage, to the lender of the money by the borrower of the money.

International fund

A mutual fund that invests in securities located outside the U.S.

Investment adviser

A person or organization that provides advice on investments for a fee.

Investment company

A corporation, trust, or partnership that invests the pooled money of shareholders in securities according to investment objectives. A mutual fund is an investment company.

Investment portfolio
A listing of all investments a person or organization holds.

Keogh plan
A retirement investment program for self-employed persons.

Leverage
The use of borrowed money, usually from a brokerage firm, to purchase stocks and other types of investments.

Limited partnership
An investment group consisting of a general partner who manages the investments of the group. Limited partners usually receive a fixed rate of return, and any loss is limited to the amount they contribute to the partnership.

Load fund
A mutual fund that charges a fee, usually between 1 percent and 8.5 percent, when shares are purchased in the fund. See no-load mutual fund.

Margin account
A brokerage account that allows you to borrow money from the brokerage firm when purchasing stocks and other investments. See leverage.

Market timing
Buying and selling securities at the beginning and end of stock market cycles.

Money market mutual fund
A fund that invests in short-term securities such as certificates of deposit, commercial paper, government securities, and bankers' acceptances.

Municipal bond fund

An open-end mutual fund or unit trust that invests in tax-exempt bonds issued by state, city, and local governments.

Mutual fund

An investment company that pools money from investors so that it can be more conveniently, economically, and efficiently managed and invested in securities.

NASDAQ

Acronym for National Association of Security Dealers Automated Quotations System. NASDAQ provides price and volume figures on securities traded on the over-the-counter market.

Net asset value (NAV)

The price per share of a mutual fund, determined by dividing the number of shares outstanding into the net assets of a fund.

New York Stock Exchange

The largest and oldest stock exchange in the United States.

No-load mutual fund

A mutual fund whose shares are sold without a sales charge, such as a front-end commission. See also load fund.

Open-end fund

A managed investment company (mutual fund) that does not have a fixed number of shares. Shares of open-end companies are sold and redeemed on investors' demand.

Over-the-counter

A market where securities that are not traded on any exchange, such as the New York Stock Exchange, are bought and sold at bid and asked prices.

Periodic payment plan

A contractual plan for investing in mutual funds. The investor makes payments to a fund on a monthly, quarterly, or other basis.

Portfolio

The total investment holdings of an individual or an investment company.

Portfolio manager

Professional mutual fund or other investment company manager who makes buy and sell decisions on securities according to stated objectives.

Price range

The high and low price of a security or mutual fund for a specific period, often called a trading range.

Prime rate

Preferential rate of interest charged by banks on short-term loans to their most creditworthy customers, expressed as a percentage.

Prospectus

The official booklet required by the Securities and Exchange Commission that describes a mutual fund's objectives, policies, restrictions, costs, and other information.

Pure no-load mutual fund

A mutual fund that does not have a front-end load, back-end load, or a 12b-1 fee.

Real estate investment trust (REIT)

A closed-end investment company that buys real estate properties or mortgages and pays dividends to shareholders based on profits from its investments.

Return on investment

The percentage gain or loss on an investment.

Risk

The chance that all or part of a person's investment money will be lost.

Sector fund

A mutual fund that invests primarily in one industry.

Securities

Stocks, bonds, warrants, options, and other investments.

Securities and Exchange Commission (SEC)

The federal agency established to protect investors.

Sell-short

To sell a security you do not own in expectation of buying it back later at a lower price to make a profit.

Shareholder

A person or legal entity that owns common or preferred stock in a corporation, or shares in a mutual fund.

Signature guarantee

A document that verifies the identity of a shareholder or person.

Standard and Poor's 500 (S&P 500)

A measure of the price change of five hundred common stocks. The S&P 500 is used as a comparison for stock market performance.

Statement of Additional Information (SAI)

A report provided by mutual funds that contains more information than what is included in a fund's prospectus.

Stock

An ownership interest in a corporation, usually represented by a certificate of ownership.

Stop order

An order that specifies a specific price at which a stock should be bought or sold.

Target price

An arbitrary price set by mutual fund shareholders to calculate the amount of monthly investments when using the DCAP formula.

Tax-deferred

The delayed payment of a tax liability on investments such as IRAs and certain annuities.

Tax-efficient fund

A mutual fund that keeps taxable distributions to its shareholders to a minimum.

Tax-exempt securities

Generally refers to municipal bonds issued by state, city, and local governments.

Term life insurance

An insurance policy that offers a death benefit for a specific period of time. The insurance premium increases as the policyholder grows older. There is no savings accumulated in these policies.

Tickertape

An electronic board that displays the price and volume of securities transactions.

Total financial plan

An investment program that covers all the financial needs of an individual or family.

Total return

A performance calculation that includes the change in an investments value plus any dividends and capital gains, expressed as a percentage.

Treasury bill

Short-debt obligation issued by the U.S. government that matures in thirteen or twenty-six weeks.

Treasury bond

Long-term debt obligation issued by the U.S. government that matures in excess of ten years.

Treasury note

Debt obligation of the U.S. government maturing in two to ten years.

Trust

An agreement where the person who establishes the trust gives property to a trustee to invest and manage for the advantage of the beneficiary.

Trustee (personal representative)

An individual or institution designated to oversee the handling and distribution of a trust.

Turnover ratio

A measurement of the extent that a mutual fund buys and sells securities.

12b-1 fee

A charge that some mutual funds assess to cover marketing and distribution expenses.

Vesting

The amount of time an employee must work for a company before the employee has the right to accrue retirement benefits.

Volume

The number of shares of securities traded during a specific time.

Will

A legal document that distributes a person's property at death.

Yield

Income on an investment, expressed as a percentage.

Zero-coupon bond

A debt security issued at a discount from its face value. No actual interest is paid until maturity.

ONLINE RESOURCES

* **Brill's Mutual Funds Interactive**
  www.fundsinteractive.com

* **College Board On-line**
  www.collegeboard.com

* **CollegeQuest**
  www.collegequest.com

* **Fastweb.com**
  www.fastweb.com

* **Finaid**
  www.finaid.com

* **FundAlarm**
  www.fundalarm.com

* **Guide to Choosing Mutual Funds**
  www.mfea.com

* IndexFunds.com
www.indexfunds.com

* Insuremarket.com
www.insuremarket.com

* Intelliquote
www.intelliquote.com

* Kiplinger Mutual Funds
www.kiplinger.com

* Morningstar
www.morningstar.com

* Mutual Fund Education Alliance
www.mfea.com

* Mutual Funds-Find- a- Fund: The Most Complete Source of Mutual Fund Information
www.findafund.com

* Mutual Funds: Investing in America's Future
www.ici.org

* Mutual Funds Net
www.mutualfundsnet.com

* Mutual Funds That Win
www.maxfunds.com

* Quicken.com
www.quicken.com

* **Quotesmith**
     www.quotesmith.com

* **Savings Bonds**

www.savingsbonds.gov

* **The Neatest Little Guide to Mutual Funds Investing**
     www.jasonkelly.com

* **Treasury Bills, Notes, and Bonds**
     www.treasury.gov

* **Wealth Watchman**
     www.wealthwatchman.com

ABOUT THE AUTHOR

Lyle Allen has been investing in stocks and mutual funds for over forty years. He received his Bachelor of Arts degree from the University of Washington in 1958 where he majored in social disorganization/criminology.

After college Allen settled in Washington, D.C., where he worked for the Cost of Living Council and held management positions with the Department of Labor. During his years in Washington, he became involved in the area of personal finance and investment matters. Since his retirement he has spent many hours developing new ways to make money in the financial markets without sacrificing safety.

In 1992, Allen developed and received a trademark for Dollar-Cost Averaging Plus (DCAP). This new and easy to use formula is a successful investment strategy he has used again and again to realize a good return when he invests in mutual funds. He is the author of five investment books, which explains how to invest in mutual funds using the DCAP formula.

Allen, an extensive traveler, makes his home in Utah with his wife and two dogs.

www.ingramcontent.com/pod-product-compliance
Lightning Source LLC
Chambersburg PA
CBHW032023170526
45157CB00002B/828